CW00434832

DIAMOND
ROUTEMASTER

Compiled by
Andrew Morgan

Published in
association
with the

ROUTEMASTER
ASSOCIATION

Capital Transport

First published 2014
ISBN 978-1-85414-375-4

Published by Capital Transport Publishing Ltd
www.capitaltransport.com

Printed by Parksons Graphics

THIS BUS

is the forerunner of the future London bus and is on trial to test its general performance and suitability.

It is of lightweight construction, embodying special features contributing to your riding comfort.

If you would like to make any comments on the 'Routemaster,' please send them to the Public Relations Officer, 55 Broadway, S.W.I.

CONTENTS

ROUTEMASTER BASICS		4
ROUTEMASTER DECADES		8
ROUTEMASTER AMBASSADORS		22
ROUTEMASTER ENTHUSIASTS		
1	Sir Brian Souter	28
2	Ensignbus – by Steve Newman	32
3	Ambassatours – by Dennis Campbell	36
4	Jorn Kolsrud	40
5	Hermann Herfurtner	42
6	Lydia and Walter Brunner	46
7	Ian Molloy (Co-owners John Doherty, Nigel Bennett)	48
8	ThisBus – by Stephen Madden	50
ROUTEMASTER CONVERSIONS		58
ROUTEMASTER COLOURS		80
ROUTEMASTER TOURS		
1	Mac Tours	88
2	The Ghost Bus	92
ROUTEMASTER PHONE		96

Left Poster displayed at the front of the lower deck of RMI.

Facing page Two of the first production RMs at the Park Royal Vehicles' factory.

ROUTEMASTER BASICS

RM585 on trolleybus replacement work at North Finchley in 1961.
(John Laker)

There were five prototypes:

RM1 built 1954

RM2 built 1955

RML3 built 1957

RMC4 (CRL4) built 1957

RMF1254 built 1962

There were 2,870 production vehicles

2120 standard length Routemasters: RM5–879, 904–1253, 1255–1452, 1521–2217 built 1958–1965

68 standard length Green Line coaches:

RMC1453–1520 built 1962

43 long Green Line coaches:

RCL2218–2260 built 1965

524 long Routemasters:

RML880–903 built 1961–1962

RML2261–2760 built 1965–1968

50 front entrance long Routemasters:

Northern 2085–2134 (RMFs) built 1964, 1965

65 front entrance standard length Routemasters:

BEA1-65 built 1966–1967

And finally, one front entrance rear engined prototype Routemaster: FRM1 built 1966

Dimensions as built

Type	Length	Width	Height	Wheelbase	Weight	Seating
RM	27ft 6½in	7ft 11½in	14ft 4½in	16ft 10in	7366 kg	H36/28R
RMC	27ft 6½in	7ft 11½in	14ft 4½in	16ft 10in	7874 kg	H32/25RD
RCL	29ft 10½in	7ft 11½in	14ft 5in	19ft 2in	8255 kg	H36/29RD
RML	29ft 10½in	7ft 11½in	14ft 5in	19ft 2in	7874 kg	H40/32R
RMA	27ft 6½in	7ft 11½in	14ft 4½in	16ft 10in	7823 kg	H32/24F
RMF	29ft 10½in	7ft 11½in	14ft 4½in	19ft 2in	7849 kg	H41/31F
FRM	31ft 3in	7ft 11½in	14ft 5in	16ft 10in	8636 kg	H41/31F
ERM	31ft 8in	7ft 11½in	13ft 9in	20ft 11½in	7660kg	O44/32R (as converted)

The dimensions of the prototypes varied slightly compared with the production batch as when originally built; for example the length of RMC4 is 27ft 3½in and its weight is 7620kg. All four original prototypes were modified since new, particularly to the frontal area, with some being rebuilt several times during their first few years. They were all modified with standard front panels in the early 1960s. Similarly, the seating capacity of RMF1254 remained unique as H38/31F.

Mechanical units

Although the standard Routemaster was fitted with the AEC 9.6 litre AV590 engine, Wilson gearbox and spiral bevel type differential, there were some variations:

628 Routemasters, including the 50 front-entrance examples built for Northern General, received the Leyland 9.8 litre O.600 engine instead.

108 Routemasters, namely the Green Line RCLs and those built for BEA, were fitted with the larger AEC 11.3 litre AV690 engine for improved performance.

Prototypes RM1 and RM2 initially received other engine types, and RM1991 was built with an AEC AV690 engine, but FRM1 was built with an ΛEC 11.3 litre AV691 engine.

The standard Routemaster suspension was coil springs with telescopic shock absorbers at each wheel position. However the RMC and RCL coaches built for Green Line work and those for BEA were fitted with air suspension to the rear instead.

The Northern General vehicles were fitted with worm drive rear axles. The RMC Green Line vehicles were fitted with intermediate high ratio rear axles (4.77 : 1 in lieu of the standard 5.22 : 1 unit) and the RCL Green Line and BEA vehicles were fitted with even higher ratio rear axles (4.08 : 1).

The position stayed reasonably static, apart from any exchanges or swops at overhaul within the Aldenham works system, until the early-1980s when withdrawals and subsequent sales commenced. For example, former Green Line vehicles then saw use in the central London area and some had their air suspension removed, and standard engine and rear axle fitted. The situation became more fluid with closure of Chiswick works and then a shortage of serviceable units due mainly to their age. Not only were engine types swopped, but different engine types were fitted initially as an experiment and then various vehicles were re-engined to keep the London fleet operational, with the most numerous being the

Cummins 8.27 litre C-series, Iveco 8.1 litre 836/1, Scania 9.0 litre DS9 engine and then latterly the Cummins 5.9 litre B-series engine.

The following numbers of Routemasters were re-engined. (It is notable that in addition to the original AEC or Leyland engine, some then had more than one from the following selection of engine types, and some engines were re-fitted to several different vehicles.)

Iveco 8.1 litre 836/1 96 RM, 1 RMC, 146 RML
Cummins 8.27 litre C-series 9 RM, 1 RMC, 355 RML
Scania 9.0 litre DS9 66 RM and 53 RML

Cummins 5.9 litre B-series 61 RM and 41 RML

Single examples of a Caterpillar, the DAF 11.6 litre DK1160VS and Cummins 5.9 litre ISBe engines were also fitted and still survive in Routemasters today, although the first two types have been sold. Those with the Cummins B-series or Cummins ISBe engine were for the first time also fitted with a different type of gearbox in place of the original mid-mounted unit, namely the Allison MT643 (fitted to 40 RM and 2 RML) or the Allison T270 (fitted to 17 RM and 39 RML). Nine vehicles (6 RM and 3 RML) were also fitted with Telma retarders.

Length of Service

The standard RM entered service on 8th February 1956 with RM1 on route 2, and RMs are still in use in London on Heritage service. After cessation of mainstream passenger service with Routemasters in 2005, parts of routes 9 and 15 were given RMs. *To date 58 years*

The prototype RMC, CRL4, entered service on 9th October 1957, and was followed by the production batch from 29th August 1962. Although moved from Green Line duties to standard bus work, they lasted in service with London Country until 5th March 1980. Technically this was the end of mainstream operation of the type until seven were resurrected by London Buses for new commuter route X15 from 15th March 1989 until 22nd November 1991. This was not quite the end, as a few remained in use as extras on route 15 up until this route was converted to one-person operation on 29th August 2003. *Total 37 years*

The RCLs entered service on 2nd June 1965 and, like the RMCs, they were withdrawn from Green Line duties to move on to standard bus work; they lasted in service with London Country until 24th January 1979. However, upon re-acquisition by London Transport, they were overhauled for use in the central area and entered service from 10th October 1980. The last one was withdrawn on 15th December 1984 and later eleven saw use on the London sightseeing operation from 1986 until 2001. *Total (not including sightseeing) 17½ years*

The initial batch of RMLs entered service on 8th November 1961 and with the delivery of a further five hundred red and green liveried examples from 1965, they continued in service until the last was withdrawn on the 9th December 2005 from the very last mainstream route, route 159. *Total 44 years*

The first batch of the Northern Routemasters (RMFs) entered service on 1st May 1964, and the final one was withdrawn on 16th December 1980. A few examples later operated on the London sightseeing tours (albeit mostly on hire), although London Coaches did purchase one example and operated it until the early 1990s. *Total (not including sightseeing) 16½ years*

The first BEA Routemaster was licensed for service from 28th October 1966 and the airport Routemasters stayed in use until the Heathrow service was withdrawn on 31st March 1979. A batch of thirteen subsequently saw service on route 175 from 11th October 1975 to 2nd September 1976, and two later saw use on route X15 from October 1989 alongside the RMCs until December 1997. Six saw use as part of the London Buses sightseeing operation from March 1987 until October 1994. *Total (not including sightseeing) 21½ years*

The unique FRM entered service on 26th June 1967 and continued until it had an accident in September 1976. However it returned to service in February 1978 and ended its days on sightseeing duties on 3rd February 1983. *Total 16 years*

Left The sole rear-engined Routemaster, FRM1, entered service in June 1967 on route 76 and two and a half years later became the first double decker in London to be one-man operated, a local route in the Croydon area being selected for it. (Roy Marshall)

ROUTEMASTER DECADES

Andrew Morgan takes a look at the history of the Routemaster in London service with decade by decade snapshots, starting ten years after the first prototype was shown at Earls Court.

1964

As the year commenced, the London Routemaster fleet was made up as follows: 1705 RM, 69 RMC, 1 RMF, 24 RML. The total number of Routemasters delivered (at 1/1/1964) was 1799. At the beginning of 1964, the following routes were operated by red Routemasters:

Monday – Friday: 5, 5A, 7, 9, 13, 14, 16, 17, 18, 23, 24, 29, 36, 36A, 36B, 37, 41, 43, 48, 58, 63, 64, 67, 69, 73, 81B, 85, 85A, 104, 117, 123, 127, 131, 141, 143, 149, 162, 207, 207A, 214, 220, 221, 238, 239, 243, 245, 249, 249B, 253, 255, 256, 257, 259, 260, 266, 267, 268, 269, 271, 272, 275, 278, 279, 279A, 281, 282, 283, 285, 293, N83, N84, N85, N86, N92, N93, N94, N99.

Saturday: 2, 5B, 7, 9, 13, 14, 16, 17, 18, 23, 24, 29, 36, 36A, 36B, 37, 41, 43, 48, 58, 63A, 64, 67, 69, 73, 74, 81B, 85, 85A, 104, 117, 123, 127, 131, 141, 141A, 143, 144, 149, 162, 162A, 173, 187, 188, 207, 207A, 212, 214, 220, 221, 238, 238A, 239, 243, 245, 249B, 253, 255, 256, 257, 259, 260, 266, 267, 268, 269, 271, 272, 275, 278, 278A, 279, 279A, 281, 282, 283, 285, 293, N83, N94, N99.

Sunday: 2, 2B, 5B, 9, 14, 16, 17, 18, 24, 28, 29, 36, 36B, 37, 45, 48, 58, 63A, 64, 68, 69, 73, 74, 78, 81, 81B, 97, 102, 104, 106A, 113, 116, 117, 123, 127, 131, 134, 134A, 141, 141A, 144, 149, 173, 181, 207, 212, 214, 220, 221, 240, 243A, 245, 249, 249A, 253, 255, 257, 259, 260, 266, 267, 268, 269, 271, 272, 275, 278A, 279, 281, 282, 285, N83, N84, N85, N86, N92, N93, N94, N99.

An additional three hundred and sixteen RMs were delivered during the year, and by the end of the year, the highest RM delivered was RM2124, taking the total number of RMs in stock to two thousand and twenty one. These were the only type of vehicle delivered to London Transport during the year; a feature that was to change over the next few years with the introduction of new types.

The replacement of the RT family by Routemasters was now under way with the trolleybus conversion programme finally completed in May 1962. During 1964, routes 3, 7, 15, 18, 23, 30, 41, 64, 100, 123, 130 group, 134 and 137 were converted to Routemaster operation with RTs, RTLs, and RTWs being made surplus. These included some routes which had been part RT/RM operation since trolleybus replacement.

March 1964 saw the first Routemaster delivered with a suffix registration, RM1866 as ALD866B, which entered service the following month. RM1865 was registered as 865DYE and there had been no Routemasters registered new with the A-suffix as the registration block 601DYE to 865DYE had been reserved and was completely used before the change to a suffix registration. December 1964 saw the registration change to a C-suffix with RM2106 being delivered as CUV106C.

Facing page RM590 at Stratford shows the first visible, and small, bodywork modifications to the type: the plating over of the lower half of the saloon ventilation grille and the blanking off of the brake cooling grilles. (Capital Transport)

Front entrance Routemaster, RMF1254, was loaned to Halifax Joint Omnibus Committee and also to British European Airways (BEA) for trials. For the latter trial, it was experimentally towing a trailer potentially for the service from the West London Air Terminal to Heathrow.

The fourth prototype, RMC4, was overhauled during the year and was outshopped on 9th December. Uniquely for an RMC, it retained the 3-piece RM style front blind box and non-opening upper deck windows.

The RM known as the Silver Lady, RM664, continued moving around different garages. This RM had never been painted since new in 1961 and as a trial, had been left in bare aluminium, but was now beginning to look quite shabby.

RMC1469 appeared in a revised livery in July. The centrally mounted Green Line bullseye had been removed and Green Line fleetnames applied forward of the advert panels, the offside route number box was removed, and the colour of the relief band was changed to a paler green. Most of the changes were later adopted for the forty-three Routemaster coaches of the RCL type, which were generally as the RMC but to the greater RML length, and were ordered later in November for delivery in mid-1965.

RM1719 was loaned to Ricardo Ltd at Shoreham-by-Sea in Sussex from January to July in the first of a series of trials aimed at reducing noise levels by adding shielding around the engine. A livery change took place from RM2063 with filled-in brake cooling grilles, blanked off heater grille below the front blind box and a flake grey relief band.

From RM1804, new vehicles were fitted with an interior illuminated advert panel on the front lower deck bulkhead. From February 1964, a start was made to fitting this feature to earlier members of the class as well. This necessitated the heater control switch being moved to a mid-window level below the new interior advert panel.

The offside illuminated advert panel was introduced in quantity from RM1923 onwards to RM2121 after experiments in 1963 with RM1577. Route 30 was converted from RT to RM and included the first Routemasters with offside illuminated advert panels. Similarly routes 9 and 13 received new RMs from the 1st September to replace older examples to enable the illuminated advert vehicles to operate on central London routes. The start of the route 137 conversion followed on 1st November and route 3's conversion from December with more vehicles so equipped.

The London Transport vehicle orders for 1965 were revised from three hundred and fifty RMs to two hundred of the longer RML type together with fifty-eight front entrance double deckers and twenty-nine single deckers. However a further three hundred RMLs were confirmed for 1966.

Outside London, the first batch of eighteen front entrance RMFs were delivered between March and May to Northern General at Gateshead. Then from October, the second batch commenced delivery and by the end of the year a total of twenty-three had been delivered.

Left The RMCs were an attempt to improve the economics of running the busier Green Line routes by having larger, and fewer, vehicles and a correspondingly lower frequency. RMC1487 is seen in Hatfield in original condition. (Geoff Morant)

RMF1254 was used at Chiswick Works to evaluate minor revisions to the frontal appearance. Adopted were the plating over of the lower half of the air intake and the lowering of the registration plate to give an unbroken line to the radiator grille surround. (Colin Curtis collection)

1974

The year was probably best remembered for the shortage of vehicles, major maintenance problems due to a lack of spare parts and a shortage of staff. The spares shortages particularly affected the newer one-person operated/ rear engined vehicles with 'no bus available' (or NBA) being a common end result. However the programme of conversions of routes to one-person operation that was started in the 1960s continued where possible.

The Routemaster fleet was now between six and sixteen years old, but any thoughts of replacement or withdrawals had been put on hold due to the unsatisfactory one-person operated new vehicles, particularly at this time the AEC Merlins, now being replaced from 1974 onwards, and the completion of the replacement of the RT family. In 1972, approximately sixty RMs received light overhauls with the intention of disposal some three years later; with all these shortages and the unsuccessful and unpopular early one-person operated types, these disposal plans were abandoned.

During the year, routes 151 and 175A were converted to RM operation (from RT), and routes 144 and 197 lost their Routemasters in favour of Daimler Fleetlines (DMS class).

At this time, all the various fleets remained virtually intact including the British Airways, London Country and Northern General, but one RML, RML2691, had been sold in September 1972 and RM1 had been sold in April 1973 (later bought back for preservation). The country area of London Transport had been separated from the central area from the 1st January 1970 and ninety-seven RMLs, sixty-nine RMCs and forty-three RCLs were now part of the London Country Bus Services fleet. The Green Line network was now operated by single deckers, and the RMCs and RCLs had been demoted to bus work except if covering for the non-availability of a scheduled Green Line vehicle.

A few RMs were written off in February 1974 after various incidents or accidents over the previous few years; these were RM50, 304, 1268, 1447 and 1659. The only Weymann bodied Routemaster, prototype RM3, was also sold in February 1974, and this became the first Routemaster to enter preservation. It was subsequently used for a number television and film appearances including for advertising commercials.

Before the year started, New Year's Eve saw another RM, RM1368, seriously damaged by a fire at Tottenham garage, taken to Aldenham works for storage pending a decision on its future. It survives today in preservation as a single decker.

All over advert liveries continued to appear during 1974, albeit a smaller number as, particularly in London, they were no longer popular. RM995 (for Bank of Cyprus), RM1255 (for Reed Employment Agency) and RM1359 (for Boulogne Chamber of Commerce) were new all-over advert liveries during the year. Ones that regained standard red livery were RM682 (for Pye), RM762 (for Esso Blue), RM1015 (for Wines of Austria), RM1285 (for Peter Dominic) and RML2560 (for Ladbrokes). Only RM1255 was left in an advertising livery at year end.

In mid-April, RMs started being outshopped from Aldenham overhaul and repaint with white roundel and fleet numbers in lieu of the traditional gold fleet names and fleet numbers.

London Country Bus Services had similar vehicle shortages, but service reductions at Amersham garage were mostly due to staffing difficulties. RMLs released here were mainly employed on heavily loaded works services from Hemel Hempstead garage.

Facing page Country Bus RML2428, seen in Hemel Hempstead in 1974, was one of those later bought back by London Transport to give the buses a new lease of life on its crew-operated routes. (Capital Transport)

The spread of the corporate National Bus Company livery continued during the year, with the first RCL (2244) being repainted in this livery in May.

At the beginning of 1974, the numbers of Routemasters in stock were:

London Transport	2122 RM, 426 RML, 1 FRM.
London Country	69 RMC, 97 RML, 43 RCL.
Northern General	51 RMF.
BEA	65 front entrance Routemasters. (later known as the RMA class)

At the beginning of 1974, the following routes were operated by Routemasters in the central London area:

Monday – Friday   2, 2A, 2B, 3, 6, 7, 8, 8A, 9, 11, 12, 13, 14, 15, 17, 18, 18A, 19, 22, 23, 24, 25, 26, 27, 28, 29, 30, 31, 33, 35, 36, 36A, 36B, 37, 38, 40A, 41, 43, 45, 48, 49, 52, 53, 55, 58, 63, 68, 69, 71, 73, 74, 74B, 76, 77, 77A, 83, 88, 97, 101, 104, 113, 117, 123, 130, 130B, 137, 141, 149, 159, 164, 171, 174, 180, 190, 196, 207, 214, 230, 243, 253, 256, 260, 262, 266, 269, 279, 281, 298, 298A, N82, N83, N84, N88, N89, N90, N91, N92, N93, N94, N96, N97, N99.

By the 1970s, the relief colour had changed to off-white and a new non-underlined fleetname (first used on FRM1) had appeared. RM1012 is seen on one-time trolleybus route 623. (Capital Transport)

Saturday   1, 2B, 3, 4, 6, 7, 8, 9, 11, 12, 13, 14, 15, 18, 19, 22, 23, 24, 25, 26, 27, 28, 29, 30, 31, 33, 35, 36, 36B, 37, 38, 40, 41, 43, 45, 47, 48, 49, 52, 53, 54, 55, 58, 63, 68, 69, 71, 73, 74, 76, 77, 77C, 83, 86, 88, 93, 97, 101, 102, 104, 113, 117, 118, 123, 130, 130A, 137, 141, 144, 149, 159, 168 (nights only), 171, 172, 174, 180, 187, 190, 196, 207, 214, 230, 243, 253, 256, 260, 261, 262, 266, 279, 281, 298, 298A, N81, N82, N83, N99.

Sunday   1A, 2B, 3, 6, 8, 9, 9A, 11, 12, 14, 15, 18, 19, 22, 23, 24, 25, 26, 27, 28, 29, 30, 31, 34, 35, 36, 36B, 37, 38, 40, 41, 47, 48, 49, 52, 53, 54, 55, 58, 59, 63, 68, 69, 71, 72, 73, 74, 75, 76, 77, 77C, 88, 101, 102, 104, 113, 117, 123, 130, 130A, 137, 140, 141, 144, 149, 168 (nights only), 171, 172, 174, 180A, 183, 207, 214, 243A, 253, 260, 266, 279, N81, N82, N83, N84, N88, N89, N90, N91, N92, N93, N94, N96, N97, N99.

FRM1 ran on Monday to Saturday route 284.

It was on routes penetrating central London that the Routemaster came into its own. RM2044 at Clapham Common heads for Oxford Circus and displays the large white roundel that replaced the gold fleetname from 1974.

1984

With the forthcoming abolition of the Greater London Council, from the 29th June a new authority named as the London Regional Transport, took over from London Transport Executive. With the ongoing reviews and the need for cost savings, the future of Aldenham and Chiswick works was at this time uncertain.

Sales of Routemasters that started in 1982 following the abandonment of the Fares Fair policy continued. In 1984, one hundred and seventy three Routemasters (157 RM, 1 RMC, 13 RCL, 1 RMA and 1 FRM) were sold; these were mostly Leyland engined examples with Simms electrical equipment and most went for scrap. Of these, showbus RM2116 was withdrawn in May and sold to the garage staff sports association and remains in preservation to this day. Another former showbus, RM1563, was withdrawn and repainted in near standard livery as a promotional vehicle for the London Bus Sales operation. FRM1 was transferred to the London Transport Museum stock.

Garage showbuses appeared in the early 1980s as garage staff adopted individual Routemasters; they were kept in excellent condition whilst still running in service and often restored to as-new condition with the restoration of features such as brake cooling grilles and gold underlined fleetnames. The staff involved even took the vehicles on their days off to rallies around the country, where some of them were successful at winning concours d'elegance competitions.

The London Country Routemaster fleet was withdrawn in March 1980 and most had been sold back to London Transport, although prototype RMC4 was retained. All of the RCLs had been purchased from London Country and after overhaul most re-entered service in 1980. Appropriately RCL2260, working on route 149, was the last one and was withdrawn from London operations after 15th December 1984.

Two all-over advert liveries on RMLs operated throughout the year and RML2492 appeared in a vivid yellow and green livery for chemist Underwoods. The garage showbuses that appeared in the early 1980s were out of favour with the management of the time by 1984. From the 50th anniversary of London Transport in 1983, the commemorative liveried RMs in 1933-style livery (RM8, RM17 and RM1933), together with gold liveried RM1983, were all repainted back to standard livery during the year.

Seventeen RMLs from Upton Park garage appeared with dedicated route branding for route 23 which was primarily aimed at visiting tourists.

During the year, route 141 was converted to one-person operation with Leyland Titans and routes 40, 47, 69, 86, 119, 119B, 161, 176 and 208 were converted to Leyland Titan operation but initially retained crew operation. Similarly, route 260 was converted to crew operated Metrobuses and routes 109, 133 and 190 were converted to crew operated Fleetlines. The result was that Routemasters were withdrawn from various garages including totally at Bromley, Poplar and Seven Kings.

RM1740 became the skid bus at the training school at the Chiswick works skid pan, replacing RT2143.

Two hundred and sixty three RMs and one hundred and seven RMLs were overhauled during the year including twenty by British Leyland at Lowestoft and Nottingham; however these took four to five months compared with just a few weeks at London Transport's own Aldenham works.

The system of separating RM and RML bodies from their sub-frames at overhaul at Aldenham works ceased after RM198 was completed in June, although RM6 and RM192 exchanged identities in October, albeit without a body lift, so that the running units of RM6 could be numerically re-united with the appropriate bonnet number.

RM1288 was rebuilt at Aldenham works with the platform to the UK-style offside and the staircase reversed to the UK nearside; it was later sent with conventional RM1873 to Hong Kong and China.

Staff bus RMA50 was withdrawn in November and was the last of the former British Airways vehicles in use in the blue and white livery of their former owner.

Seventy-one RMs were equipped during the year with a radio equipment system known as BUSCO for the 36 group of routes. Another feature to appear during the year and to become common was the L-shaped advert as applied to the offside between decks advertising space and down the staircase panel.

At the beginning of 1984, the total numbers of Routemasters in stock with London Transport were: 1882 RM, 51 RMC, 503 RML, 35 RCL, 48 RMA, 1 FRM.

At the beginning of 1984, the following routes were operated by Routemasters in the central London area:

Monday – Friday   1, 2, 2B, 3, 4, 5, 6, 7, 8, 8A, 9, 11, 12, 13, 14, 15, 16, 16A, 19, 21, 22, 23, 24, 25, 27, 28, 29, 30, 31, 35, 36, 36A, 36B, 37, 38, 40, 41, 43, 45, 47, 48, 49, 52, 52A, 53, 63, 65, 68, 69, 73, 74, 76, 77, 77A, 86, 88, 109, 113, 118, 119, 133, 134, 137, 141, 149, 159, 161, 171, 172, 176, 180, 190, 207, 208, 237, 243, 253, 260, 266, 279, N90, K1 (Mon and Thur only), K2 (Tues and Fri only).

Saturday   1, 2, 2B, 3, 4, 5, 6, 7, 8, 9, 11, 12, 13, 14, 15, 16, 16A, 19, 21, 22, 23, 24, 25, 27, 28, 29, 30, 31, 35, 36, 36B, 37, 38, 40, 43, 45, 47, 48, 49, 52, 52A, 53, 63, 65, 68, 69, 73, 74, 76, 77, 77A, 86, 88, 109, 113, 118, 119, 133, 134, 137, 141, 149, 155, 159, 161, 171, 180, 190, 207, 208, 237, 243, 253, 260, 266, 279, N90, K1, K2.

Sunday   2, 2B, 3, 5, 6, 7, 8, 9, 11, 12, 13, 14, 15, 16, 19, 21, 22, 23, 24, 25, 27, 28, 29, 30, 31, 35, 36, 36B, 37, 45, 47, 48, 49, 52, 52A, 53, 63, 65, 68, 73, 74, 77, 77A, 86, 88, 113, 118, 119B, 133, 134, 137, 149, 159, 161, 171, 207, 208, 237, 243A, 253, 260, 266, 279A, N90.

In the 1980s a number of garages refurbished RMs to 'showbus' condition for rallies and similar events in addition to running in regular public service. RM737 from Harrow Weald garage is seen at Queensbury. (Capital Transport)

1994

At the beginning of 1994, seven hundred and sixty one Routemasters remained in stock with London Buses (243 RM, 13 RMC, 502 RML and 3 RMA); however, by the end of the year, this figure had dramatically dropped as this was a significant year in the history of buses in London.

1994 was the year when the majority of the main operating subsidiaries were privatised; the final company, South London, followed in January 1995. The tendering of all routes had commenced in 1985 and by 1994 the whole of the London route network was operated on a tendered basis.

Following the tendering of route 159, the route passed solely to South London and the London Central share of the route ceased. South London introduced a dedicated livery for route 159 on the RMs of red and cream. The last RM, 2217, was repainted in January with the fleet of twenty-five being completed by the end of the year. During the autumn, this fleet received fluorescent strip lighting, internal repaints and some DiPTAC features.

Route 38 was operated by Leaside Buses which from December started applying its Routemasters with dedicated route details, similar to those already seen on route 73 vehicles.

Re-registrations of Routemasters continued; oddities included DRM2516 being re-registered WLT516, RM994 becoming VLT89, and in reverse, RM1324 regaining 324CLT. The first RMLs and RMCs were re-registered during the year; however, all regained their WLT and CLT registrations later in their lives. Some companies kept the registrations from RMs that had acted as cover during the RML refurbishment programme and that had become surplus upon the completion of these works to the RML fleet during the summer.

Early in the summer, the RML refurbishment programme was completed; in total, five hundred RMLs were completed with the work being carried out by South Yorkshire Transport (later renamed Mainline) in Rotherham, TBP in Birmingham, and Leaside Buses in north London. The last few RMLs were re-engined ahead of being refurbished so that the fleet was now Cummins or Iveco engined. Only RML903 and 2760 remained unrefurbished in original condition and fitted with AEC engines.

As the preparations to the privatisations continued, all surplus vehicles, including all spare RMs, were disposed of, leaving thirty RMs as a reserve fleet and the forty-six RMLs that were then leased to BTS Coaches and Kentish Bus for routes 13 and 19 respectively. The newly created reserve fleet was transferred in December to Hatfield to be stored and looked after by University Bus for London Buses. All RM training vehicles were withdrawn and sold. In total one hundred and twenty seven RMs and two RMCs were sold during the year. Interestingly, many of the RMs that were sold during this year went to scrap dealer PVS in South Yorkshire, and although they have gradually been scrapped, some of these still remain there in 2014.

On the 14th December, RM1992 became the last RM to be sold by London Buses.

The newly privatised companies quickly wanted to stamp their identity and started to repaint their vehicles in new liveries; the Stagecoach London RML fleet were repainted with cream relief bands, gold fleet numbers and gold East London fleet names. RMC1461 was repainted into full Green Line livery by Stagecoach and it made its debut at the Routemaster 40 celebrations on 24th September. Routemaster 40 was a one-day event held jointly at Covent Garden with the London Transport Museum and at the Royal Victoria Docks by the Routemaster Association. Some ninety-six Routemaster vehicles participated in this event and it saw all types of Routemaster attending and taking part.

At the beginning of 1994, the following routes were operated by Routemasters in the central London area:

Monday – Friday   6, 7, 8, 9, 10, 11, 12, 13, 14, 15, 19, 22, 23, 36, 38, 73, 94, 98, 137, 139, 159, 390.

Saturday   6, 7, 8, 9, 10, 11, 12, 13, 14, 15, 19, 22, 23, 36, 38, 73, 94, 98, 137, 139, 159, 390.

Sunday   13.

Additionally, the Original London Sightseeing Tour was operated with Routemasters at this time using a mixture of open top, and closed top, RMs, ERMs and RCLs. The ERMs were rebuilt from open top RMs in 1990 to become one-bay longer and thus thirty-one feet eight inches long.

Also, by this time, it was common for many routes to be operated in the evenings by one-person operated doored vehicles.

Above This open-top RM was a frequent visitor to Centrewest's routes in the 1990s and is seen in Oxford Street turning into New Bond Street on a temporary diversion. (Capital Transport)

Left Route 13, operated by BTS in its light red livery, became the last normal Routemaster route regularly operated in Sundays. (Capital Transport)

2004

The year before 2004, the final chapter in the mainstream operation of Routemasters in central London had commenced; with the success of off-bus fare collection, the large increase in the numbers of passengers, the introduction of bendy buses, and the reduced benefit of the conductor, the Routemasters were deemed less of a necessity in central London.

The strong disabled lobby and the successful introduction of low-floor buses made the Routemaster look old fashioned. Although there was fierce opposition, the decision had been made and in a little over two years, the 600-strong Routemaster fleet was gone.

At the beginning of 2004, five hundred and sixty-six Routemaster remained in stock by the various London operating companies (128 RM, 4 RMC, and 434 RML); however, by the end of the year, this figure dramatically dropped further.

At the beginning of 2004, the following routes were operated by Routemasters in the central London area:

Monday – Friday   6, 7, 8, 9, 12, 13, 14, 19, 22, 36, 38, 73, 94, 98, 137, 159, 390.

Saturday   6, 7, 8, 9, 12, 13, 14, 19, 22, 36, 38, 73, 94, 98, 137, 159, 390.

Sunday   8, 13, 14, 19, 38, 94, 137, 159.

In 2000/2001, a final renaissance of the Routemaster had occurred with forty-nine RMs being acquired by Transport for London with the initial forty-three being refurbished by Marshall's at Cambridge.

The Routemaster 50 anniversary year was notable with a large event taking place in July at Finsbury Park, and numerous vehicles carried the 'RM50' logos. Notable vehicles restored for the Routemaster 50 event included RML3 with original front and RMF1254 back to original condition. Other notable vehicles at the event included RM470 returning to the UK from Germany and RM809 from Sweden.

First London repainted RM1650 back to 1977 condition as Silver Jubilee SRM3, albeit now with Euro II Cummins B-series engine and Allison gearbox, hopper windows and many other modifications.

Two other special liveried Routemasters operated on route 19 to commemorate 175 years of London bus operations. These were Great Northern liveried RM25 and Shillibeer liveried RML2524.

RM275 appeared in an all-over advert livery for the film Harry Potter and the Prisoner of Azkaban; RM2217 later appeared in this livery as a replacement, although neither were used in normal passenger service.

Many last days, or even the days leading up to the final day, saw special operations over the routes before conversion from the Routemaster type; many guest vehicles were included to commemorate not only the end of Routemaster operation, but also the last conductors.

The route conversions during the year were as follows:

Route 94 on the 23rd January
Route 6 on the 26th March
Route 98 on the 26th March
Route 8 on the 5th June
Route 7 on the 2nd July
Route 137 on the 9th July
Route 9 on the 3rd September
Route 73 on the 3rd September
Route 390 on the 3rd September
Route 12 on the 5th November

The 3rd September conversions saw the last AEC engined Routemasters operate in daily service (RML903 on route 390, and finally a few hours later, RM5 on route 73) and the end of ninety-two years of AEC engined buses in service in London. Route 390 was introduced as the western end of route 10 on 1st February 2003 and so lasted under two years with Routemasters.

This left routes 13, 14, 19, 22, 36 and 159 as the only Routemaster operated routes at the year end.

RM1 made a visit to Buckingham Palace on the 22nd November to participate in a celebration of 'Good British Design' icons.

By the end of the year, tender documents had been released for the proposed heritage Routemaster Tourist Routes that were later launched in November 2005 as short versions of routes 9 and 15.

By now, special Routemaster fleets were being formed by private companies, including the main London operators. The Go-Ahead Group regularly used their vehicles on special operations to several events including to the Chelsea Flower Show and Wimbledon Tennis events.

Another Go-Ahead vehicle, RML2317, was re-engined from Iveco to Scania after transfer from London General to neighbouring Metrobus, repainted to Lincoln green for various uses including private hire work and for the route between East Grinstead and the Bluebell Railway before that railway's extension.

Go-Ahead also re-registered a large number of their Routemasters and sold the registrations off ahead of the vehicles themselves being withdrawn and sold.

Unusually the disposal of the surplus Metroline Routemasters was handled by that company themselves, and First London and London United also sold some themselves, but later joined all of the other companies by selling them to dealer Ensignbus.

RML2516 was rebuilt with a rear door after accident damage as DRM2516. It is seen on the special service between Victoria and the Chelsea Flower Show which employed Routemasters (among other types) after mainstream service with them had ceased. (Vernon Murphy)

ROUTEMASTER AMBASSADORS

In the 1960s and early 1970s, Routemasters were on numerous occasions used for goodwill and trade visits overseas. James Whiting has been researching TfL archives for stories from some of those trips.

Between 1950 and 1975, the traditional open platform London Transport double decker took part in around 50 overseas tours to promote Britain or British companies and very often more than one bus was involved. The periods of the visits ranged between one week and six months and included a number of towns and cities in Europe, North America and Japan. The first such trip to involve a Routemaster was at the beginning of 1961 when one vehicle, RM546, went to Basle in Switzerland for a British Week.

It was often the case, as with this first trip abroad with a Routemaster, that the driving was not done by a regular London Transport driver. Three members of London Transport's engineering staff were given charge of the bus, all of whom were trained to LT's driving standards and held PSV licences. Unusually, though, it had been agreed that the driving in Basle would be done by drivers supplied by the local public transport authority. On most of the trips that followed, London Transport's own staff did all the driving, not only to and from the destination. Conductresses were supplied locally as it was obviously important to have someone on board with good local knowledge. They were however given proper London Transport uniforms.

The following year saw the first visit of a Routemaster to North America, when one of the latest 30ft long versions, RML898, went to San Francisco. All of the driving this time was done by members of the three-strong engineering staff. The Americans really took to the Routemaster and during the bus's nine-day stay almost 10,000 passengers were carried on a free one-mile circular tour of the shopping district that ran for six hours a day. Many people commented on the comfort and the moquette-covered deep-cushioned seats and were surprised to learn that the bus was a standard vehicle no different from others in service in London, a sentiment often repeated on overseas tours. In 1963 another vehicle from the same batch was sent to Philadelphia and further trips by Routemasters to the States followed, as well as a number to Europe and Scandinavia.

In most of the places visited by Routemasters on their excursions abroad, the rule of the road was to drive on the right and it is recorded that in one North American city, an intending passenger was spotted trying to get into the driver's cab. It seems he thought this was the entrance as he was used to boarding on that side. When told of his mistake, he remarked 'I thought the door was a bit small and rather high up'.

Another factor that resulted from the unfamiliarity of double deck buses in many of the cities was the presence in some of overhead tram wires. The staff on the vehicles had to check clearances for these, and other possible overhead obstructions, before doing any carrying of passengers. Another hazard that came to light was that of small children trying to put their arms out of the upper deck windows, which in some cases could have brought them in fatal contact with tram wires. Consequently, where this risk was present, the upper deck windows had to be locked shut.

In the second half of 1965, Japan was added to the list of countries when RM 2214 made an 11,000 mile boat journey to take part in a British exhibition in Tokyo. It was a big success there, with its Japanese conductors, so much so that four years later no fewer than eight Routemasters made the trip for another British event in Tokyo, the largest number of London buses to go on an overseas tour at the same time.

During 1967 came the first trip of a Routemaster to Canada when two RMLs left England in March bound for Montreal. It was also the longest of any of the officially-organised Routemaster trips abroad and was for a six-month long World Fair, Expo 67, held between April and October. A five-man crew accompanied the two buses, one of which remained in North America after the fair to travel to Pittsburgh, of which more later. Both vehicles arrived back in the UK during December, by which time they had been away from home for nine months.

Overleaf RMs 2158 and 2159 in Amsterdam for a British Week in May 1965. The same two vehicles were used for a trip to Milan later in the year. (Colin Brown)

Left RM2214 being offloaded after its long journey to Japan for a trade fair in 1965. (TfL Archives)

The RMLs that visited Montreal were sponsored by Brooke Bond and were fitted with special lights above the upper deck windows to satisfy local regulations. (Bill Godwin)

The Canadian tour was not without incident. When both buses were offloaded on 4th April, they were driven directly to the Canadian Steamship Warehouse and banned from being driven because the Quebec authorities did not recognise the British driving and PSV licences. All who were going to drive the buses had to take a series of tests, which were successfully passed just in time for the scheduled start of the service on 28th of the same month. Also required were Quebec registration plates, as the buses could not be used in Canada with their UK registrations. Getting these required a series of interviews with the licensing authority. Later in the year, the London Transport officials complained that the local authority in Montreal seemed to regard the two London buses as more trouble than they were worth.

There were also a number of issues between the crews and the sponsor of this trip, Brooke Bond Canada Ltd, which in addition to the poor local preparation for the buses included the sponsor taking most of the limelight and the buses and crew sometimes being treated like extras in their publicity campaign. There were also some major disagreements with flexibility of scheduling to take account of the huge demand, with the sponsor insisting on its right to keep to the agreed schedule come what may. This even applied in the latter part of the operation, when the staff of the Montreal bus undertaking went on total strike for 30 days, placing even more pressure on the free London buses. Major delays were experienced on the route, with on one occasion the normal 20-minute journey taking two and a half hours. A one-hour journey time was common during the strike.

A hazard that soon became apparent was the unreliability of bridge clearance signs in Montreal. Taking a double decker bus abroad requires extra awareness of overhead obstructions and relying on the signs was not advisable. An underpass used on the daily special service in the city was signed as having a clearance of 14ft, whereas in reality it was 14ft 7½ins – which made the difference between being passable and not. On the other hand a clearance marked as 15ft 3ins turned out to be 14ft 5½ins – just enough, but very tight.

As was clear at an official level from the moment the buses arrived, the almost universal popularity of buses from London experienced in other places visited was not experienced in Montreal. A minority of passengers, while willing to accept a free ride, voiced criticism of anything British. There was also a certain level of rowdiness, encouraged in the view of the London Transport crew by the short skirts worn by the hostesses at the specification of the sponsor. The four 'hostesses' in Montreal had been employed directly by Brooke Bond. No special traffic or parking arrangements were made for the buses and the drivers had to contend with bad parking and very narrow clearances in places. At the end of the six months in Montreal, the two buses had carried nearly half a million passengers despite all the problems, and much favourable comment from passengers was received. The crew stated in their report of the trip that the Routemasters had been 'pillars of reliability' during their six-month stay and gave 'tangible evidence of quality British engineering in everyday operation'.

A total of 51 special journeys were also made during the stay, including one for an American Indian tribe in full and highly colourful ceremonial dress from Montreal to the Caugnawaga Indian Reservation near the city. On another occasion, a special party of guests was taken to the Delson Museum of the Canadian Railroad Historical Association in connection with the presentation to it of the British Rail A4 class Pacific locomotive 'Dominion of Canada'.

RML 2548 spent ten days in Toronto in October for a 'British Week' there. Accidents on overseas tours were fortunately quite uncommon, but on its way to Toronto, the bus was hit in the rear by an American coach. The damage to the bus included forward movement of the staircase, bent rear framing and extensive panel damage. Local assistance was obtained for replacing the panels and the bus was completely repaired in the course of a day. Because of the delay to the bus, a police escort was provided for part of the rest of the journey to its destination, which it reached in time for a 10am parade the following morning after a quick wash for both the bus and the crew. During the stay there, a number of special guests were carried including Canadian prime minister Lester Pearson. Its reception in Toronto was somewhat warmer than from some of the people encountered in Montreal. Its main work in Toronto was again a circular service in the main shopping and commercial district. It was helped at busy times by a locally owned and older London double decker of the RTL class dating from the early 1950s.

After its time in Toronto, the next stop was Pittsburgh, USA. This was another addition to the original plan and the trip here was made at the request of Gimbels department store, who had organised a 'Great Great Britain' fortnight. Here the bus and crew received a particularly warm welcome, but the warm welcome of the people of Pittsburgh was not matched by the weather. On its first night there, the bus had to be parked in the open at temperatures as low as 15 degrees F. But little starting trouble was experienced the following morning, the engine firing occurring within 30 seconds of ignition. Also there to add to the British flavour were a policeman from Coventry and the Lambeth Town Crier.

One of the last tours made by a Routemaster was of five European countries between mid-September and the beginning of November 1973 to promote a London Entertains event that was organised by the British Tourist Authority for the following February. The countries visited were Belgium, Holland, Germany, Switzerland and France. In Brussels, the police had to be called in to control the crowds attracted by the bus despite bad weather. The bus was also well received in all the other countries it visited on the tour and featured in many newspaper articles and television programmes.

Facing page The Routemasters sent on the overseas trips were equipped with Gibson ticket machines fitted with special plates to issue commemorative tickets.

A locally employed 'London conductress' stands beside a 'dolly' stop for the special Routemaster tours. She would have looked rather out of place conducting a bus in London. (TfL Archives)

ROUTEMASTER ENTHUSIASTS

SIR BRIAN SOUTER

Sir Brian Souter is the chairman of Stagecoach, one of the largest bus companies in the world. He set up the company in 1984 as a small operation in Perth and he soon saw the potential of the Routemaster for some of his early operations. Here he speaks to James Whiting about his connections with Routemasters for almost thirty years.

I bought the first Routemasters for the Stagecoach bus company in 1985. We had begun operating in the Perth area with old Bristol buses, which were becoming difficult to maintain owing to difficulties in obtaining spares. Also, they had outdated 'crash' gearboxes which were challenging to drive. We did not like the early designs of rear engined double decker. They were prone to break down and were expensive to maintain. Some of the routes we had were conductor operated anyway and so a front entrance bus with doors was not necessary. I saw in the Routemaster a bus that was highly reliable, fuel efficient, easy to drive, popular with passengers and a bargain at the price being asked by London Transport who were selling large numbers of them at the time. I bought the first ones for £1500 each including the tyres. I wanted to evaluate the buses for possible use when bus services were deregulated the following year. I had my eye on Glasgow when the bus market was opened up and felt that Routemasters would be ideal for competing in the city with the established Scottish Bus Group. This large group also bought Routemasters for some of its services after keeping an eye on our operation.

The very first one taken into our fleet was used for country bus service. I had a door put on the back because people on the route were used to doors and didn't like an open platform, which can be draughty at times. When deregulation came, I began running services in Glasgow with unmodified Routemasters under the name 'Magicbus' and the Glasgow people just loved them. Our service, with two routes, soon became profitable. In those days there was very little off-bus ticketing and so having the drivers take fares as passengers boarded slowed things down a lot. By running Routemasters and using conductors, we could operate a higher frequency with fewer buses and provide passengers with quicker journeys.

However, I did not go into direct competition with the Scottish Bus Group by simply copying their busiest routes. I went out and researched roads that were well populated but without a bus service. I found out later that these roads used to have bus services when buses were, like the Routemaster, narrower and shorter than modern buses. The Scottish Bus Group buses could not go down them, but the Routemaster could. The first winter that we were running to Glasgow's Castlemilk was a very harsh winter and everyone said that these old buses would not be able to keep going. In the event, when the snow was at its thickest, we were the only buses running

From October 1986 to April 1992, Stagecoach operated Routemasters in Glasgow under the Magicbus name, although Routemaster operation lived on for another year as it passed to Kelvin. A collection of RMs were gathered for the new operation that commenced from Deregulation Day. Additionally four RMFs and two RMAs were added to the fleet in Glasgow for use on other services, contracts and schools. (Andrew Morgan)

there. The Routemaster handled very well, especially when there was a good load of passengers on board. I did some driving myself in those early days, and also more recently. With Magicbus I would stand in if we were a driver short, but more recently it has been to keep in touch with what is happening.

The Routemaster's running costs were very low. I could buy a secondhand engine for £300, a secondhand gearbox for £100, and so on. Also, because the staff union had not reckoned on conductors coming back to buses, there was no up-to-date agreed union rate for a conductor. With unemployment high at the time, the quite low wages paid to conductors were more than covered by the savings in depreciation and in operating and maintenance costs compared with a modern driver-only operated bus. I supplemented the conductors' wages with commission on tickets sold, giving them a stake in the success of the services.

With bus service deregulation in place, Stagecoach expanded enormously and I was always on the lookout for other areas of Britain where we could usefully introduce Routemasters. They were introduced in Carlisle, Bedford and Corby. In Corby they even took business away from the taxis. I would only put in Routemasters if the local management agreed as I do not believe in imposing decisions on them. One place where I thought we could do well with Routemasters was Southampton, where we operated services as part of the Hants & Dorset company, but the local management did not like the idea.

When bus services in London were opened up to private companies under contract to Transport for London, Stagecoach successfully bid for services in east and south-east London. The east London operation included two Routemaster services, the 8 and the 15. London services are not deregulated so we did what we were contracted to do, but if it had been my decision I would have kept the Routemasters and run them on biofuel. I drove on route 8 shortly before the Routemasters were replaced by modern vehicles. I do not rule out operating Routemasters again somewhere – possibly on a sightseeing service at a coastal resort. Until late 2012, Stagecoach kept a small fleet in reserve ready for any good opportunity to use them. Latterly a number were exported to Canada and the remainder passed to various Stagecoach companies around the group.

I have also had a Routemaster converted for personal use. It is one of a batch designed in the mid-1960s for carrying passengers and luggage from central London to Heathrow Airport via the M4. There are now three bedrooms upstairs, with living quarters downstairs. It serves as a caravan that I can drive around for family holidays. The fact that it has doors coupled with its smaller size compared with modern double deckers makes it ideal for this. Also its modified design for airport work makes it excellent for motorway driving. The furthest south we have been so far from our Scottish base is Oxford.

It seems to me that there is also potential for India or China to build Routemasters to the original design for local use. Compared with modern vehicles, the Routemaster is lightweight anyway but knowing what they have achieved in India with weight reduction on other motor vehicles, they could probably knock a ton or more off the design's weight. The question of weight is one that I have taken up with bus manufacturers. Modern buses are typically around 12 tons in weight whereas the Routemaster is around 7 tons, one of the reasons for its fuel efficiency. Yes, modern buses are larger, but it seems to me there is still scope for buses to be lighter than they are.

Facing page Preserved Routemasters generally are repainted back to London red livery, but two exceptions are Clydeside liveried RM835 and Kelvin liveried RM910. The latter RM operated for Kelvin Scottish between 1986 and 1992. (Richard Godfrey)

ROUTEMASTER ENTHUSIASTS 2

STEVE NEWMAN – ENSIGNBUS

Ensignbus took the plunge in buying Routemasters when they were being sold en masse by London operators at a time when there were few takers for them. Within a couple of years, however, the decision proved to be a very good one. Steve Newman tells us about the company's experience with RMs and RMLs.

August 2003 saw the first Routemaster to be acquired by Ensignbus. RML2743 was collected from Stagecoach London at Waterden Road, Stratford and was quickly used for promotional material. Ross Newman actually collected it as we were very familiar with the East London route 15 and almost knew the buses and had a bit of a soft spot for them. At the time the London operators were looking where they could possibly dispose of 45-year-old open platform double deckers, but Ensignbus had already agreed to take many of them as it did with many other classes of London bus. No one could imagine what would happen next – there was very little interest in the first acquisitions from route 15 and only a very few had been sold by the time the second route came off. At Ensignbus, it was seriously questioned whether we had we made a mistake and dropped a clanger!

They were difficult to price, and the initial batch was very difficult to sell. The second batch came from the remnants of route 11 from London General. By this time though it had already been decided to take all the batches from the major operators despite the difficulty in selling them.

The decision was taken to acquire and store the Routemasters with a view to the longer term so far as sales are concerned. The Routemaster sales activity and publicising that they were available were tasks which fell to me. I often dealt with the areas around the edge of the standard Ensignbus operations and I had experience of dealing with the media, which would prove useful as the worldwide interest later grew. Another important issue was that floor space was required by the operators quickly after a route was converted and Ensignbus could offer to collect vehicles as they became available. Most were collected direct from the garages, and this became ever more important to stop items being stolen. Radios were often removed at Purfleet after the vehicles had been collected.

Selling Routemasters was in many ways more like selling coaches than buses; every owner wanted different things done. I would often ask prospective owners, "What do you know about RMs?" as an introduction and then give them a class history if required. Many owners-to-be thought that RMLs had been chopped and extended, and wanted the 'pure' RM. Preservationists often wanted the RMs, but others really wanted the RMLs as there had been very few RMLs available until then. Owners who wanted to do conversions generally wanted the longer RMLs for the extra space. The registration plate was also important, as many of the RMs had been re-registered before sale, whereas most of the RMLs still had their original plates.

The vehicles had already been graded in condition, the good to the not-so-good – A, B, C, D – with the factors being engine type, overall condition, scratched glass, length of MOT, etc. Prices originally ranged from £9500 for a Stagecoach Scania to £6500 for a London General Iveco. Some prospective owners would already have strong views on what they were looking for, whilst others had the strangest pre-conceived ideas on what they wanted! For example, for some it had to have head lamp surrounds whilst completely ignoring whether it started or not and smoked – it had to be shiny, have front wheel trims and destination blinds. Some wanted a particular number, former London Country ones, original body, overall adverts, ones they had ridden on in service, or simply just had memories of them, and these owners knew what they wanted. The strangest reason was when one was selected because the buyer liked the graffiti on the bus, but the customer is always right! I would often suggest that they checked the gearbox or the engine, or looked underneath it but, no, they liked the destination blinds, and on such reasons individual buses were often chosen!

The worst part of the sale was that owners were always keen for a test drive. You could define new owners in various ways. There were the professional drivers with psv or hgv experience who had no problem with the length but they would often drift to the left, hug the kerb and hit a few; they might be professional drivers but they had never driven a half-cab before which visually tends to make people drift to the nearside. These drivers were cautious when they left the yard for the first time but confident and willing to listen and learn. Then there were those with no bus or large vehicle experience. The vehicle would usually require some work to be completed

before leaving the yard, even if just battery or brake charging, but also repaints, MOTs were carried out, so the vehicle would not always be collected straight away. At this stage it was often suggested that some professional instruction was taken before collecting the bus ... some listened and some did not!

Then there were those that had driven a Transit van sized vehicle in the past, had no caution, would ignore all advice, and knew it all. I would suggest that they get used to the vehicle in automatic before trying anything else, but they would often not listen – terrifying is an understatement! The worst ever experience was with a repainted vehicle and after a demonstration, the driver then proceeded to forget every rule of the road: he did not give way – and an articulated lorry screeched to a halt inches from the drivers' door and then had to back up – as the know-it-all driver turned right, but not hard enough so that he scraped the front nearside of the newly repainted bus along several concrete bollards, chewed up the nearside wheel trim, damaged the nearside wing, and then reversed into a lampost column. The driver was then furious with me as I immediately took over driving the bus back to the yard, where he was offered a full refund as there was no way he was going to be allowed to leave the premises to take his new acquisition out on the road and possibly hurt someone. His wife then appeared from the saloon and said, "Didn't he do well" ... ! Luckily this new owner learnt from his experience and took some lessons before he collected his Routemaster.

I considered that we had a duty of care to give new owners guidance, rather than to let them 'collect and go'. As part of this, new owners were soon taught the Routemaster's width, length and how to position it on the road. Bus driving was assumed by many to be simple, but it is far from it. Some owners took over an hour for their test run, others just fifteen minutes, and only the one new owner previously mentioned was not allowed to take it with him. Routemasters were often collected on Saturdays and Sundays when it was quieter on the roads. Another new owner was confused with which pedal to choose … and there are only two in a Routemaster! Others ignored stop signs, road markings, and could not place the bus in the correct position on the road. The steering would catch out many new owners and indeed me as well – not all the Routemasters are set up the same way and locks can be very different.

I have a marginal preference for the Cummins C-series engined Routemasters in terms of driving, but the Cummins B-series is a favourite as an operator as it is easy to maintain and mechanically similar to the Dennis Dart fleet. The Scania engined Routemaster is very reliable, and an example of this is that the majority of the six RMLs that were flooded at Carlisle in January 2005 were reinstated. The Iveco engined Routemaster is the least favourite, although most came from some of the nicest of garages and were cosmetically and mechanically good; it is not an ideal mechanical set up with the fuel pump on the offside of the engine for example. Whilst some were notoriously sluggish others were quite sprightly. Vehicles from Putney had a waiting list of potential owners, generally for historical reasons and the good condition of the vehicles.

It was notable that there was initially very little UK media interest and it was the international media that first made contact, with the first television interview being carried out for Kuwait TV at the Frog Island storage site. This then mushroomed with probably over 100 television interviews, on-line interviews, radio, road tests for motoring magazines and culminating with live broadcasts throughout the last day on the 9th December 2005 from Purfleet. The BBC London local news programme took over one of the barns at Purfleet with a live outside broadcast for their entire early evening programme, including the weather forecast from the cab

of a former Arriva RML. Peter Newman and myself were also interviewed on another one, and RCL2220 rounded off the show driving into the dark as the credits rolled. The day had started with American West Coast evening news and followed to Sky Sunrise and Good Morning America. There were TV crews on site for the entire 24 hours – this alone must have had millions of viewers all focusing on the events being broadcast from Ensignbus at Purfleet. It was obvious that the media wanted the story of the icon from bus people, with a backdrop of withdrawn ones and personal stories and recollections rather than press releases.

So the initial risk to buy all the main batches of RMs and RMLs ended up with them all finding homes. Only a handful have been sold for scrap and none of these came from Ensignbus. Including several that subsequently returned to Ensignbus, just over 25% were sold overseas. Out of the 347 Routemasters that were acquired from the bus companies and re-sold by Ensignbus from 2003 to 2006, they can be divided into three main categories with approximately 50% going to private individuals, approx 25% going to promotional non-psv companies and the remainder going to operational use for heritage services, weddings, etc.

The market for corporate hires has increased, and like many operators, Ensignbus now has additional Routemasters in the fleet. With others in our collection, and some awaiting restoration, we are now proud owners of one of each type. The last RM in service, RM54, is now part of the heritage fleet.

We tried to acknowledge the historical significance of vehicles (for example liveries, overseas tours or vehicles of numerical note) to the point that they were always pointed out to prospective owners wanting one for preservation, thereby ensuring that any significant vehicles did not go abroad if at all possible. Mid-way through the Routemaster sales, Ensignbus realised that they would not be stuck with any Routemasters as demand was far outstripping supply and, at the time, values were increasing, but most of the later demand was from overseas. Therefore we wanted to ensure that serious preservationists had the opportunity of acquiring a Routemaster, and the idea of the RM Raffle was born. At the time, the average price for a Routemaster was £8,000 each and the vehicles to be included as part of the raffle were sold for £2,000 each plus VAT plus the cost of the tyres.

Originally there were twenty vehicles set aside to be spread around the United Kingdom, but after a massive positive response, this number was increased to thirty-two. The number thirty-two was picked as it corresponded with the number of years since the company had been founded. The numerous applications received were sifted through to find the right owners to look after them and to preserve them for future generations. A number of the successful owners are still in regular contact, and are still thankful for the opportunity.

As part of the original agreement, none of these thirty-two vehicles could be re-sold until three years had passed, unless back to Ensignbus. Two or three were subsequently sold on to make a profit immediately after this date passed, and this left a bit of a bad taste as it was not in the spirit of the idea. However, the majority of the vehicles are now well preserved examples, have encouraged some interesting websites to be formed for many others to enjoy or provided use for others, and have given many other people around the UK enormous pleasure. The time of the RM Raffle in mid-2004 was probably the start of the main media interest.

On maintaining the sales stock, the hardest items to source were the destination blinds. Everyone wanted a set of blinds for their bus and not all buses came in with blinds! Front wheel trims, head light trims, seating moquette and mechanical parts were all sourced without too much problem. We even have a spare original AEC engine.

Selling Routemasters overseas added a level of complication, with the sorting of permits and shipping all taking time to resolve, although these are usually the buyer's responsibility. Vehicles to Canada require special attention including steam cleaning underneath prior to shipment. Different countries have different requirements before being passed to shipping companies. There can often be problems afterwards, for example the 4.0 metre EU height restriction, certification in a particular country, or just time zone differences that have to be dealt with. Ensignbus though has a lot of experience of exporting buses, and usually knows what is required and knows to ask the right questions to make sure it all goes smoothly.

Selling the brand of the Routemaster was without doubt a fascinating interlude in our normal onward sales, such was the interest both from buyers and the media. I think the proudest thing for us is the fact that despite the numbers we received and the usual need to rob at least one of a class in a big batch, we did not scrap a single Routemaster. Even the real 'basket cases' that had been donors at the back end of depots, we collected and sold on, sometimes for future static use, other times for ground up restorations. That any such vehicle in any condition could be found a home says a lot about the regard that this particular bus is held in by so many people the world over.

In the following pages, some of the proud overseas owners of Routemasters bought from Ensignbus write about their experiences with them.

ROUTEMASTER ENTHUSIASTS 3

DENNIS CAMPBELL, AMBASSATOURS, NOVA SCOTIA

Nova Scotia based Ambassatours is now the largest owner and operator of Routemasters; it is nearly twice the size of any Routemaster operation in the UK. Dennis Campbell is the President of the company and introduces us to his operation.

I bought my first Routemaster (RM 937) in 1998. I had connected with Ted Brakell (Omnibus Sales) through Lionel Moss. While RM 937 was my first Routemaster, it was my fourth bus in our fleet since starting the company in 1994. Today we have twenty-five Routemasters in a fleet of seventy-three buses, based in Halifax, Nova Scotia. The Routemasters are the favourite buses I have owned. We have purchased most of our Routemasters from Peter and Steve Newman at Ensignbus. They have been a total pleasure to deal with and are a large part of our success in my opinion. We have used our Routemasters primarily in seasonal Hop On Hop Off daily sightseeing operations primarily for the cruise ships arriving into Halifax Nova Scotia (fifteen units), Saint John New Brunswick (eight units) and now Sydney Nova Scotia (two units).

In 2006 the doctor told us that my 78 year old mother had breast cancer and was not likely to make it to the age of 80. Wanting to do something for the cause, six years ago we decided to paint one of our Routemasters pink in support of Breast Cancer Research. We then thought why just one; why not paint eight pink? So we proceeded to paint eight Routemasters pink. Everyone thought I was crazy and they are possibly correct. We spent over US $50,000 in pink paint and decals and had a very unique and bright fleet of pink Routemasters. We offered the Canadian Breast Cancer Foundation $1 for every person that travelled on these eight large mobile billboards promoting breast cancer awareness and anticipated donating about US $15,000 at $1 per passenger in the first season. We were all pleasantly surprised when our first year donations were over US $33,000. To date, we have donated US $185,849 in just three seasons. We have since trademarked and licensed the concept and it is now a separate company called Big Pink Sightseeing. Our first licensee location was Vancouver followed by Portland Oregon, Charlottetown PEI and most recently New York. We are presently in discussions with many American and Caribbean locations about becoming a licensee for Big Pink Sightseeing in support of Breast Cancer Awareness. By the way, my mother turned 85 in 2013 and is living well and independently, albeit still with breast cancer, but due to medical advances today, medication keeps the disease from progressing.

We have created Big Pink Sightseeing Routemaster (Sunstar 1:24 scale) models and (Welly 1:74 scale) toys to help create more interest, awareness and sales resulting in donations to the cause at $1 donated per toy bus sold. The pink Routemaster Welly toy buses are being made available for sale in Walmarts in Canada.

RML880 became well known for carrying London United livery from 1989 to 2006, but RML881 remained red throughout its London service life and then gained a pseudo London General livery after sale in 2004. In 2005 it was sold to Ambassatours in Nova Scotia, where it initially retained this livery, before gaining their now standard pink livery. (Paul Bateson)

While we continue to invest in and take good care of our Routemasters, they have continued to pay dividends every year we have owned them. Routemasters are the only buses we own which now seem to be appreciating in value. Of the fleet of twenty-five, all but two have been repowered with either Cummins B or C series engines. The two oddballs are RML2316 (the only Routemaster ever repowered with a Caterpillar engine) and RM937 which is still working great today with its original AEC engine. We did buy RML2465 with an Iveco engine but found that underpowered and have since replaced the Iveco with a Cummins engine. Our head engineer John

Bartlett, tells me that if we keep maintaining them as we do (along with making and rebuilding our own parts) the bodies will outlive him and me and our children. When it comes to Routemasters John is mostly self taught and has become one of the foremost experts on them in Canada, advising various locations across the country on Routemaster maintenance and care.

For the record, the numbers are:

RMs: 937, 1018

RMLs: 881, 2281, 2309, 2314, 2316, 2328, 2329, 2332, 2336, 2365, 2373, 2465, 2507, 2525, 2534, 2553, 2578, 2651, 2664, 2673, 2675, 2677, 2689

Ambassatours in Nova Scotia now has the largest fleet of Routemasters, and many have received various modifications for their new operator. On these pages are three examples. All the RMLs in this fleet have been fitted with a new right hand side doorway as seen on RML2525. RML2673 uniquely has had the platform lowered and platform doors fitted; note also the opening windows fitted to the rear emergency exit. (Paul Bateson)

RML2328 was repainted into a black livery in 2006 and then used to promote the Ipswich waterfront. In 2010 it was sold to Ambassatours and the livery was quickly adapted to advertise Durty Nelly's, with the pink paintwork being applied to the upper deck in due course. It is seen at Pier 21 at Halifax in Nova Scotia. (Paul Bateson)

ROUTEMASTER ENTHUSIASTS 4

JØRN KOLSRUD, NORWAY

Nine Routemasters are now based in Norway including three RMLs. In 2004, a group of Anglophile enthusiasts from Hamar in south east Norway bought a piece of London's history for themselves. Jørn Kolsrud is one of the group and tells the story so far.

RML2610 is now named Olde Liz (after being properly and ceremoniously baptised in London Pride ale) and is a very active retiree based in Hamar, a town some 75 miles north of Oslo in Norway.

RML2610 was brought to Norway by ferry from Newcastle on 11th September 2004 by thirty London enthusiasts; it is now used as wedding bus and party bus in the inland of Norway. Olde Liz has become something of a celebrity in the Hamar district, and during sunny days in the summer, she is also used as a pub down by the beautiful Lake Mjøsa.

When she was registered with the Norwegian road authorities a discussion took place concerning the safety of the vehicle on Norwegian roads. One of the inspectors believed it to be essential to move the platform over to the right hand side because the bus was not designed for right-hand traffic! Needless to say, the new owners sweated excessively before they persuaded the authorities to register her as "worthy of preservation".

Another oddity is that the authorities apparently think Norwegians are significantly fatter than residents in London; while RML2610 was registered for seventy-seven (seventy-two seated and five standing) passengers in London, she can only carry fifty-four passengers around the shores of Lake Mjøsa.

As all Routemaster owners know, some consideration is needed when planning a route. In Hamar, for example, only one route is possible under the railway if Olde Liz is to access the lower part of the town centre, and even then there is a clearance of only 2 cm! One of the drivers had a laconic comment the first time we drove her under there: "Just drive on! She's too high only the first time!" In spite of that comment we can assure all Routemaster lovers that we take very good care of RML2610. During the winter of 2008/2009, we even had her back in the UK for a total makeover at BusWorks in Blackpool. They did a fantastic job on her.

Because of the snow and the cold weather (sometimes below 30°C) Olde Liz goes into hibernation from 1st October to 1st May every year. During the summer season she is really busy, and we have great joy and fun with her. So, if you are coming to Hamar in Norway, you will probably be able to see her in summer operating for many years to come.

Facing page This atmospheric view of RML2610 was taken on 12th May 2009, the day after Olde Liz returned to Norway after refurbishment at Blackpool, and was posed alongside lake Mjøsa in Hamar. Additional lights and smoke were provided for the photo shoot to create this dramatic result. (Gunnar Klingwall)

ROUTEMASTER ENTHUSIASTS 5

HERMANN HERFURTNER

In July 2004, Hermann brought RM470 from Germany to the Routemaster 50 celebrations in London and was one of the highlights of the event. Afterwards he added two RMLs to his collection and has continued to use them for various contract work and tours throughout the country.

Until 1994 I only collected small vintage cars, but then I got the idea to buy a Routemaster bus. All my friends said that I was now totally crazy..... so I contacted London Transport and in November 1994 bought RM470.

To be street legal in Germany, I had to convert it to a height of 4.0 metres. The roof was removed and the bus equipped with a 'sunroof' which could lift up. Through co-operation and working with one of the most famous newspapers in Germany, my bus quickly became known and the bookings for advertising purposes followed very quickly. Orders for day events and road shows also followed. So over the next two years, I bought some different English buses, including RML2605 in December 2005 from Ensignbus and RML2663 in September 2006 from a local dealer.

Contracts were carried out for numerous clients including T-Mobile, Southern Comfort, Ladival, Nissan, MTV Television, RTL Television, Vodafone, Audi 24 Hours of Le Mans, Ikea, Dunlop tyres, Evian water, Nokia, as well as various film productions, fairs, highway openings, the European Song Contest, cycling events and much more, as seen in the accompanying photos.

We even attended the Routemaster 50 anniversary in 2004, with our RM470 in Finsbury Park; it was a wonderful experience.

In almost 20 years of work with the Routemaster buses they have proved to be very reliable. For operations up to 8000km for each promotional tour, the vehicles have never let me down and are always very reliable.

For health reasons, I had to reduce my work with the buses some time ago, and I have now sold RM470 and RML2605 in 2010 and 2011 respectively. However I still hope to complete many interesting jobs during the next few years with my very beautiful RML2663.

RML2605 was used in July and August 2010 for a promotional tour for the then new Nissan Juke SUV car in Germany, Austria and Switzerland. Bizarrely the upper deck floor was covered with sand, and with the addition of deck chairs, bean bags and a few plants, there was an instant beach on the upper deck of a Routemaster. Is there anything that a Routemaster has not been used for? (Hermann Herfurtner)

RML2605 was appropriately named 'Silver Lady' and is seen without its roof on an action day in 2009 for the newspaper 'Neuss-Grevenbroicher Zeitung' in Neuss.

Hermann Herfurtner's garage in Neuss in 2009 with, left to right, Leyland PD3 PHJ951 (which was sold in 2010 to the Jesada Technik Museum near Bangkok, Thailand), RML2668, RML2605, RM470 and a minibus.

RML2605 undertook a promotional tour in 2008 for T-Mobile when it covered 7,000 kilometres across Germany. It is seen here on the isle of Sylt in northern Germany.

RM470 and RML2668 are seen at an open day in 2008 at a large steel mill in the city of Krefeld where they were used for visitor transport.

ROUTEMASTER ENTHUSIASTS 6

LYDIA AND WALTER BRUNNER, BAVARIA

RML2490 left the streets of west London where it latterly operated on routes 7 and 23 and was taken to Bavaria in south eastern Germany where it is now a mobile restaurant; Lydia and Walter Brunner tell their story.

It all began in 2004 when our English friends read an article in 'The Times' about the plan to sell off Routemasters. Knowing of our interest in all things English they suggested that we buy one.

Valery, our friend Philip's wife, was entrusted with choosing from a considerable number housed at the Ensignbus depot in Purfleet, whose quality ranged from "in need of considerable attention" to "very good", with prices pitched at 2500, 7500 and 9500 pounds, depending also on the engine – Iveco, Scania or Cummins.

So we authorised buying one of Valery's choice and set about navigating our way through the labyrinthine ways of German bureaucracy (mainly because of the 4.38 metre height) for a permit to bring it to Bavaria. News of the trip spread, and our English friends were inundated with offers to be passengers, eventually taking their son, daughter and her boyfriend, with me completing the passenger list. Later a hitch-hiking student joined us.

Philip had to drive – amazingly on an ordinary UK driver's licence – and after a cursory 15 minute lesson from an Ensign driver the 650 mile journey via Harwich and Cuxhaven began. The next task was, sadly, to remove the roof (according to German regulations only 4 metres are allowed) and instal one which could be lowered during transit and raised as required.

The interior received fridges, sink and related paraphernalia to allow for catering, including re-arranged seating at tables upstairs and downstairs.

Some re-painting and general refurbishment followed and RML2490, now also known as 'Piccadilly Queen', registration number ER-PQ 1 H, was ready for its new life in and around Nuremberg: hosting wedding and birthday parties, stag and hen outings; corporate and VIP promotions by a leading Bavarian brewery; international sporting events such as the 2006 World Cup; and in 2012 giving an appropriately English send-off for Nuremberg's Olympians as they headed for the London Olympics (where they were Gold Medal winners for the German hockey team).

And in February 2013 it greeted on the runway of Nuremberg Airport the first flight by City Jet from London's City Airport. 'Old connections die hard'.

We are pleased to report that no real problems, either with any relevant authorities, or driver misjudgement as far as driving on the right is concerned, have been encountered. Walter had to take an exam to obtain his HGV licence; and a licensed bus driver from the village is employed when more than eight passengers are taken on a trip. As far as maintenance is concerned the compressor and quill shaft were successfully replaced,

sourced through Imperial Engineering. Other parts such as window rubbers were obtained in anticipation of future use through the good offices of the Routemaster Association. Repairs are carried out by a local lorry specialist workshop, although they sometimes find it difficult to trace the problem; the compulsory braking check is done in May and the TUEV (MOT) in November by qualified engineers, with a clean bill of health given every year so far! It has also proudly displayed the Historic Vehicle sign for the last four years.

ROUTEMASTER ENTHUSIASTS 7

IAN MOLLOY (CO-OWNERS : JOHN DOHERTY AND NIGEL BENNETT), DUBLIN

Based in Dublin, RML2575 is one of five RMLs now in Ireland and is preserved by a group of three enthusiasts. Ian Molloy recounts the story of this RML and how it came to be three-hundred and sixty miles from London.

With the very rapid withdrawal of Routemasters during the period 2003 to 2005, many people realised the great significance and finality of what was taking place, and some (including two enthusiast friends and myself) decided to acquire one for preservation. This in itself was indeed creating a challenge for ourselves, as we were living in Dublin! We were aware that those based at Putney garage had been maintained very well and were in especially good condition cosmetically. So we decided to approach dealers Ensign of Purfleet, as they had apparently acquired all the ex-Putney RMLs. As it turned out, many other people also had special regard for the Putney buses, and most had already been sold when we enquired. At that stage, both RML 2517 and 2575 were still available options, and we chose 2575 mainly on the basis of my preference for the fleet number (it divides by 25 evenly – no remainders!)

Directly following the conversion of route 13 on 21st October 2005, we collected RML2575 from Purfleet and brought it back through central London to Putney Heath (via route 14). Our collection was almost three months to the day from when it was withdrawn with the conversion of both Putney-based routes 14 and 22 to OPO. We then brought it via the M1/M6 to Holyhead docks in Anglesey

from where it was exported to Ireland. Customs officials on duty at the port seemed somewhat bemused at the sight of the RML queuing up to board ship for Dublin.

RML2575 was built in 1966 with an AEC engine, which was replaced in the early 1990s with an Iveco unit in common with many of its sisters. Following its acquisition for preservation, it has been both re-panelled and re-sprayed into London General 2005-style livery / logo. The original UK registration JJD 575D is still carried (i.e. neither of the Irish formats "ZV" nor "66-D" has been substituted).

Since re-spray, we often take RML2575 out for manoeuvres on roads around Dublin. Needless to mention, it gets noticed by very many people. June 2009 provided the opportunity for it to pay a courtesy visit to Galway where it overnighted at the local Bus Éireann garage. Later that year (October), it returned to London briefly, parking overnight at the Plough Lane overflow facility for Putney garage. The opportunity was taken to drive it over routes 14 and 22 which it had worked almost continuously for 39 years since new in 1966.

A Dublin sightseeing bus overtakes RML2575 with its locally produced destination blinds for London route 38 (Darren Hall).

ROUTEMASTER ENTHUSIASTS 8

STEPHEN MADDEN, KEN BRUCE, CHARLES NOVE AND ALAN DEDICOAT

What is it like to own and manage a Routemaster Hire Company? Stephen Madden writes about ThisBus, a company that currently own six RMLs which are available for weddings, funerals, christenings, bar mitzvahs or just fun days out.

From a very early age I'd spend every Saturday criss-crossing London, camera in hand, photographing Routemasters. On Sundays, I'd cycle from my Kingston home the mile to Norbiton Garage, sometimes Fulwell, Putney or Mortlake, and stare admiringly at the lines of glistening RMs, never thinking I'd own one. But fast-forward many years and this suddenly seemed vaguely possible. At BBC Radio 2, I was among like-minded friends (love of transport and radio seem so often to come together). Charles Nove and I used to muse wistfully that "One day, we'll own a Routemaster". Ken Bruce agreed, and so did Alan Dedicoat, but for a long time it was just a joke between us about the unattainable.

We were determined, but never came close. The nearest we came was when Reading Mainline were disposing of their fleet in the year 2000. They were available for £6-7,000 each. Charles and I went to Reading to look round. Engineering Manager Jeff Stoute was very helpful, but our bank accounts weren't. We knew we couldn't get that kind of money together, and besides, where would we store the thing? And there was the small question of irate wives to consider – but the idea never went away. We knew it was possible, because a broadcasting friend, the legendary Mike Hurley, had done it. He'd bought his in 1985 from a man in a pub in Bradford. Apparently, the man said "Pssst, wanna buy a Routemaster, yours for 2000 quid?" The deal was done, and all Mike had to do was meet his wife from work with the cheery phrase "You'll never guess what I've just bought". She must have calmed down eventually, though probably not much. Mike encouraged us (not that we needed much encouraging).

In spring 2004 I read that the dealer Ensignbus had launched a generous scheme to help would-be bus preservationists like us. With certain conditions, 32 newly-withdrawn Routemasters were being made available to 32 groups for a knock-down price. Like a broadcaster's nightmare, we had just missed the deadline. I rang Ensign anyway, and Steve Newman couldn't have been more helpful. He threw us the lifeline that we could get in on the coat-tails of the Ensign 32 scheme. Without this generous offer to honour that knockdown price, the idea would have stalled right there. But it looked like it was really going to happen.

So the Broadcasters Bus Consortium was born. The four of us met in the glitzy showbiz surroundings of Heston Services on the M4 in July to discuss plans. The atmosphere at the time was feverish, with every group who had half a chance of buying a Routemaster nabbing suitable storage space all across the South. I managed to reserve us a place in a facility on the Surrey/West Sussex border – we had to start paying rent on the empty space immediately, or lose it.

In the December, true to his word, Steve Newman invited us down to Purfleet to choose from a shortlist of nine – mostly Tottenham RMLs, recently withdrawn from the 73. On Friday 17th December, Charles, Ken and I met in monsoon rain at Ensign's yard to select our bus. Nabbing the best one wasn't easy – our first choice had been sold "ten minutes ago", so it came down to a straight fight between RMLs 2518 and 2394. It was hard to choose between them, but 2394 had a now-rare Leaside Buses radiator badge! But for that badge, it could so easily have been 2518.

Collection Day was Sunday 9th January 2005, mild and sunny at first. One of the complications of group ownership is geography – unless you live next door to each other or to where your bus lives, it's a logistical challenge to do anything, because your cars always end up in the wrong place, etc. With families along for the great occasion as well, Collection Day required five cars and at least one taxi! Having paid for the bus, we headed for the nearest diesel station, and spent £105 topping up (a full tank of fuel for an RML costs £185 at 2014 prices).

By the time we reached the Surrey/Sussex countryside, it was pitch dark and raining heavily, and it had been a long day. As the dark of a January night closed in, Charles somehow managed to peer through the gloom and the rain on unlit country roads just enough to find the farm, which he'd never even seen before.

Owning a Routemaster is exciting and fun, but it's not easy or cheap. 2394 was cantering towards MoT expiry (in March), so we took it to Guildford and it failed on brakes. Fortunately, it didn't fail on the horn, which had become intermittent on the journey to the MoT station – somehow it hooted at the key moment – but the brakes were headache enough. This kind of thing eats money. We soon discovered a brake accumulator was leaking and many attempts to fix it ended in a new accumulator, which I collected from Imperial Engineering. They weigh a ton and they're not cheap. We pumped money in, got the brakes fixed by Ward Jones at High Wycombe and got our Class 5 MoT. 2394's real Achilles' heel has been starting in wet or cold weather. It starts fine in good weather, and runs fine once it's warmed up, but still hates starting in the cold and the damp.

We wanted to get the bus looking respectable and had various frightening quotes for the work. In the summer of 2005, we were introduced to Brian Simmons at a rally, saw some of his work, and instantly booked 2394 in with him to have the exterior done. We drove direct from the Amersham Running Day in October to Brian's yard, and two months and a substantial cheque later, the bus was looking like it did when new in 1966. To this day, Brian and his son Dave do all our bodywork. They are amazing.

All this was getting expensive. Having naively budgeted for the purchase price plus the monthly rent plus the occasional diesel, we soon realised having a bus was a good way of losing vast amounts of money. We had to find a way of clawing it back. People kept asking us if they could hire it for a day out and we explained we'd need to be a fully-licensed operator, which we weren't. Our options were (a) Just keep pouring money in, or (b) Become an operator and maybe get some income. We chose the latter.

And that was when the Broadcasters Bus Consortium became ThisBus.com. Becoming an operator is not for the faint-hearted and it took an unbelievably long time, too. You need to change the Taxation Class of the vehicle from "Historic" back to "Bus". That'll be £500 p.a., please. To do that you need Hire and Reward Insurance, and that'll be £1200 a year. Oh, and Breakdown Insurance. Oh, and you'll need an Operating Base. And a highly-respected Maintenance Contractor. And legal lettering. And Public Liability insurance. And you'll also need a Transport Manager or CPC holder, along with much else.

At long last I'd saved up enough money to take the PCV Driving Test (Charles and Ken had got theirs, pre-bus, in late 2004). I passed at Yeading – in another Friday monsoon – in November 2006. So now we had three PCV drivers, which helped.

David "Sheps" Sheppard was a colleague of mine from BBC Radio Berkshire, with a young lifetime steeped in bus preservation. Being young and keen, he felt he could cope with the learning needed to be our Transport Manager, and we all thought so too. Huge weighty files of case studies started to arrive. Exams followed. Sheps passed early in 2007. We now had our Transport Manager and that summer we got our Operator's Licence. It had seemed like an eternity, but we began taking bookings and haven't looked back.

We specialise in Private Hire all over the London area and occasionally beyond. Early on, we took on work much further afield, but soon realised that at 40 miles an hour you spend half the day getting there and half the day getting back. The Routemaster can do sedate motorway travel, but it's not meant for it. Besides, it's slow, boring and very noisy for the driver. Most of our work is weddings, but we've done birthday outings, Christenings, trips to the coast, bar mitzvahs, office bashes, corporate hospitality, photo shoots, film work and parades.

Weddings are, in theory, straightforward and uncomplicated, but no two jobs are alike. Some involve a simple trip from the church to the reception venue, but we've found reception venues can be in the oddest of places, like at the far end of a one-way street with no room for turning a bus around. We've had more than one job where it's been necessary to reverse down the entire length of a street. One Surrey wedding had its reception at a barn complex in the middle of the West Sussex countryside, at the end of a long and winding track, off a long and winding single-track lane. The owners of the venue were keen to strike up further business with us, but, nice though they were, we're not going back!

Early on we learnt to treat 18th Birthday celebrations with, er, caution. On a cold January night we picked up the assembled high-spirited throng from Brook Street to take them to Chislehurst. We had been assured that they would be well-behaved, which 95% of them were. The parents had even arranged to chaperone the whole thing by driving behind us in their Honda S2000. What could possibly go wrong? Much to their embarrassment, the 5% who had over-indulged needed rather too many unscheduled stops along the route. It was a long, slow journey to Chislehurst that night, and the clearing up went on till dawn. Oh, what fun! Never again, we vowed.

The shortest job we've done so far was done as a favour for a friend-of-a-friend, and involved transporting the cast of a West End play to a nightclub at Park Lane, a short hop away. Our guests included Dame Judi Dench, Belinda Lang and Peter Bowles – I remember being surprised that Peter Bowles was eating a bag of crisps when he boarded and, very politely, asked if it was OK to sit upstairs. Er, yes.

A charity job for BBC Children In Need in 2008: Roger French and his family had won a Children In Need auction prize of an all-expenses paid day out in London, with lunch on HMS Belfast etc. Roger had bid a very significant amount of money for the day and we hope we did them proud. Here RML2394 stands at the London Eye. On the platform are the French family with full ThisBus crew – Alan Dedicoat (extreme left) and Ken Bruce (extreme right) with, in the foreground, David Sheppard (left), Charles Nove (centre) and Steve Madden (right). (Stephen Madden collection)

A typical wedding. Here, RML2261 attracts the customary attention at the Parish Church in Roehampton village, while we ready ourselves for the short trip to the reception at the Telegraph Inn on Putney Heath. There's often a lot of milling-about at weddings, and it's usual for many of the guests to want their picture taken with the bus. This was a job I drove, with life-long friend Bob Stroud conducting. (Stephen Madden)

Another early client was comedienne Jackie Clune, who got married on the hottest day of 2008. The long journey to the reception in central London was accompanied by the piercing sound – in the driver's ear – of the low coolant alarm. As it happened, this was merely an electrical malfunction and the only solution was to disable the alarm. Matters were topped off nicely by one of the guests insisting on getting off the bus in the City to visit the Gents in a nearby pub, the problem being that you can't stop a bus just anywhere, so how was he ever going to find us again? He may still be out there somewhere. In fact, parking and general traffic restrictions in central London are the bane of our lives, but we have to plan ahead as meticulously as possible and build such things into our plans. Most Saturdays are affected by demonstrations and marches, not to mention London's football teams playing at home – try picking up at Fulham Town Hall when Chelsea are playing at home at the same time and the streets are closed.

Our most difficult day by far must have been 18th December 2010, when the blizzards came at just the time when all our buses were setting out from the yard. It snowed and it snowed. After a while, it became obvious there was nothing we could do but accept all buses had to turn round and make it back – if they could – through the appalling conditions, and fortunately our clients all understood. Amazingly, RML 2408 managed to get through to its job, having set out for Henley a little ahead of the deluge. RML 2408 is made of stern stuff, and so are our crew, Richard and Andi. They were frozen but stoically unfazed and managed the required two shuttle-trips from the hotel to the church high in the Chilterns and back again. They got home, after a long day, at around 2230.

One of the most unusual things we've done was to provide the bus for an all-expenses-paid day out for a listener who'd bid a huge sum for the privilege as part of the BBC Children In Need auction in 2007. So one Sunday in May 2008, we met up with Roger French and his family and friends to give them as memorable a day in London as we could manage. I hope he felt he got his money's worth.

Sometimes it's hard to remember we came into this to have fun, so it's good to remind ourselves occasionally. There's no doubt that one of the best things about owning buses is taking part in Running Days. We've had great times running in service at Slough & Windsor, Amersham, Leyton, Uxbridge, Sutton and regularly at Cobham. There's nothing quite like transporting an appreciative crowd along a recognised route, which is why we so much enjoy providing a shuttle service for the annual Towersey Festival in Oxfordshire over the Bank Holiday weekend each August. In 2006, I'd observed that the festival-goers had to walk the mile-and-a-half to Thame, the nearest town, for food etc., and remarked that "what these people need is a shuttle-service". Very quickly, Ken produced a sample timetable (he's good at that sort of thing) and we applied for a limited licence to run as Route 73 for the four days of the Festival. The popularity of the service has grown year-on-year ever since.

One job we won't forget was the London Mayor's New Year's Day Parade in 2009. A PR company hired us as a mobile base for handing out free gifts to the swarming crowds of frozen onlookers. Collecting the gifts took much of the previous day, so one day's work very quickly became two. On the day, Charles and I had a very early freezing start, but the job went fine. Until Pall Mall. We'd been stopped, waiting for the parade to move again, for a couple of minutes, when there was an almighty bang. The 1916 Dennis fire-engine behind us had suddenly leapt forward and impaled itself on 2394's rear. We'll never know what caused it. It was miraculous that nobody

was injured, but the back end of the bus was a mess. Even the staircase had been shunted forward slightly – it was a very expensive repair, and we were without the bus for three months.

Fortunately, we had acquired RML 2261 the previous month and had it hastily readied for service. 2261 is a highly significant bus, in that it was the first of the production batch of RMLs in 1965 and went on two separate tours of the USA to promote British business, once when new and then again after first overhaul in 1972.

We never turn clients away if we can help it, and if we're full up we re-direct clients to other companies. In among the weddings, parties, PR events, product launches and film work, we have undertaken jobs that are plain bizarre – like the 300+ Antipodeans dressed as Santa Claus on a pre-Christmas binge (below). Another of the most memorable jobs was when we were brought in by another company to help provide several buses for the World Skills Conference at the ExCel – there were 35 Routemasters in all, running in convoy. If things take an unpredictable turn, like your merry Australian passengers suddenly decide they like the sound of a wine bar rather than the originally-planned Liverpool Street Station, all you need do is flag down a passing Police car – instantly, an offer of a Police escort to the new destination! Everybody loves Routemasters.

We've recently taken a party from a Jewish school on a sightseeing tour of Central London on the express understanding that we wouldn't take them near places of Christian worship, which limits the options a bit – kindly avert your gaze, or you'll suddenly see traces of St Paul's Cathedral. Only once have we had to sign a confidentiality agreement. There are rumours this was a birthday party for a member of the Royal Family, but I couldn't possibly comment. And yes, they booked us again later.

With mixed feelings, we've provided transport for several funerals. The hardest one of these was that of our own Jill Ponsford, who worked unpaid as our ever-enthusiastic marketing person. She died suddenly after a short illness in May 2013. She was 42. Her funeral, on a hot day in June, was attended by RML 2335 and a massive turnout of ThisBus staff. We still can't believe she's gone, and have dedicated RML 2261 to her memory.

We now have six RMLs, 2335 (below) being the most recent acquisition. This had a full refurbishment before entering service in September 2012 and is our current "pride of the fleet", being essentially the same vehicle that entered service as a green Country bus at Godstone in October 1965. Like most Country RMLs, it was never body-swapped, so still has its original body, B2335, and during its refurbishment some of the original green paint came to light.

ROUTEMASTER CONVERSIONS

As the typical and instantly recognisable London bus, and especially after the publicity when they were withdrawn from mainstream London service in 2005, Routemaster buses are still very popular for uses other than carrying passengers on a conventional bus route.

In the United Kingdom, for example, they have been converted to various formats including for promotional work, either for advertising or corporate hospitality, static offices, mobile bars and food outlets for use at events. At the time of writing, there were approximately fifty-six vehicles converted and available for this use, with seventy-five per cent of these being the longer RML type.

The nature of these conversions can vary from the quite basic to the major reconstruction of the vehicle, and this can entail some serious modifications to the bodywork or even a complete rebuild to form some interesting and clever examples. Unfortunately the more severe the conversion work, the more it becomes increasingly unlikely that these vehicles will ever be rebuilt back as a traditional London bus and carry passengers again.

RML2479 was converted by South East Coachworks for a campaign for Coca Cola in advance of the 2012 London Olympics. The RML travelled around the UK promoting the 'Nominate a Future Flame' campaign which culminated in the announcement of 1300 names of young people that would later run alongside the Olympic flame in the build up to the Olympics. The opening panels revealed a VIP area upstairs with a DJ deck which could open upwards and out to entertain the crowds. The interior photo above shows the opening panels in their closed position (South East Coachworks).

RML2542 has been converted into an entertainment and viewing bus for use at polo matches for George Mountbatten, the 4th Marquess of Milford Haven. The upper was rebuilt to part open top with seating fitted under the retained roof sections at the front and rear. The lower deck is now a bar area complete with kitchen area, sink, fridge, television and DVD surround system. (South East Coachworks)

Right After life in London, RM388 operated with Kelvin Scottish in Glasgow from 1986 to 1992 and was later acquired by Yorkshire Belles. It was rebuilt with an open rear staircase and is now used for tours and private hire work in the York area. (Andy Izatt)

Superdrug has owned RML2741 since 2005 and it has undertaken several tours for various promotions for this company. The interior of the Superdrug Beauty Bus, as it is known, is equipped with make up areas (beauty stations) and soft seating. (William Swain) (South East Coachworks)

Left RM1158 was converted to open top and rebuilt with a left hand staircase and right hand platform in lieu of the original design when acquired by a North Carolina based owner in 1998. In 2009 it was subsequently acquired by The Boat & Bus Company in Toronto where it is used on their sightseeing tour alongside their eight other open top Routemasters. (Nigel Eadon-Clarke)

Above RM1788 was originally exported to Ontario in 1986 and operated by Piccadilly Bus Tours. After 2003 it passed to two other owners before being acquired by Virgin Mobile Toronto. In 2009 it was rebuilt with a raising section to the centre of the roof, a platform door was fitted and the bus was repainted into a vivid red based livery for Virgin Media. (Nigel Eadon-Clarke)

RCL2259 spent several years in Belgium only to return to the UK in 2009 and pass to clothing shop White Stuff. As part of the promotion it was undertaking, a competition was held to win this Routemaster and The Kindness Offensive was the lucky winner. Although RCL2259 has a red frontal area, the rest of the vehicle has had this eye-catching and colourful vinyl wrap applied. Internally it has a few seats fitted and the spare space is used for a variety of uses in connection with the events undertaken by this volunteer organisation. (Andrew Morgan)

The Charles Wells Brewery based in Bedford have owned RCL2240 since 2001. Although it was rebuilt as a convertible open top vehicle for use on the London Coaches sightseeing tours, it has retained its roof with its new owner. Internally it has been fitted with a bar and seating. (Andrew Morgan/Malcolm Burgoyne)

Left RML2752, owned at the time by TfL, was used by a French performing arts group. They used giant puppets, and one of them was paraded around London on the upper deck of the bus on a evening tour to promote the shows, which took place on Horse Guards Parade. (Russell Young)

Above RML2284 underwent an extensive rebuild during 2004-2006 when it was converted to single deck with the upper deck and staircase removed and a side door fitted in place of the familiar open platform. The work was carried out by The Coulsdon Old Vehicle & Engineering Society. At the same time, the main mechanical units were replaced and a later version of the turbocharged Cummins C series engine was fitted mounted to a ZF 4HP400 fully automatic four speed gearbox with torque converter and integral retarder. The braking system was converted from hydraulic to a full air brake system. Internally the finishes were completed with railway rolling stock fixtures and fittings and a total of eight seats were fitted. (Richard Godfrey)

After service with Arriva London on route 159 until 2005, RML2333 became a static office in north London at a car sales forecourt. It then became the One Stop Beauty Bus where you can receive various beauty treatments on site either upstairs or downstairs in this unique salon. (Andrew Morgan)

One of the more unusual conversions for promotional work is RML2464. It has been used for such purpose since it was sold to Masters Exhibitions & Shows in 2005 and has seen regular use by the Bank of Scotland and NatWest Bank. Having been converted to part open-top in 2005, it has now been fitted with a very odd looking new roof. In late 2013, this RML was rebranded in the corporate colours for NatWest. (Richard Denny)

Former Stagecoach London RML2496 was stored after withdrawal from London service and then exported to Coach USA in 2010. It was then substantially rebuilt by the Perfect Body & Fender Company of New Jersey on to a Freightliner chassis, converted to left hand drive and to open top. After being used briefly in New York, it was transferred to the Chicago Trolley & Double Decker Co. (Coach USA)

In 1984, two RMs were dispatched by London Buses to China in the hope of potential sales to that country. RM1288 was converted to left hand staircase and right hand platform at London Transport's Aldenham works before leaving the UK, but was further rebuilt in 1985 with two entrances/exits. It then travelled to Shen Zhen and Guangzhou in China before returning to Hong Kong and was later acquired by Citybus who further rebuilt it several times. By the summer of 1992 its bodywork had been converted to pseudo vintage style and it was now open top. Twenty years later it is the only one still in use in Hong Kong and it is seen in Kowloon in November 2010. (Nigel Eadon-Clarke)

RML2538 had latterly been owned by Transport for London as one of their own fleet of Routemasters. After leaving London service, it passed through several owners and in 2012 became the *Routemonster*. It now has been fitted downstairs with a fully equipped kitchen and bar and upstairs with a seating area for twenty-six that can be used as a restaurant or even a conference area. (Andrew Morgan)

The M&M's World London shop is situated in Leicester Square and opened on 13th June 2011. As you walk through the entrance doors, you immediately see the remains of RML2561. Now with its mechanical units removed, most of the upper deck removed to fit under the ceiling, a large hole cut through the bodywork, and LED screens fitted, you can walk through what was the lower deck of the bus to reach the rest of the shop. Although it remains in London, this is a sad end to a London bus. (Capital Transport)

In 2012 RML2457 was rebuilt as The Rosebery; it now has a cocktail bar downstairs, and upstairs an eighteen seat dining area with the centre section of the roof lifting up. The interior is finished in oak, leather and shagreen. It is now available for weddings, birthdays, anniversaries, exclusive events or other special occasions. (The Rosebery)

The Wellcome Collection in Euston Road wanted to put on a Curiosity Roadshow in 2013 and what better vehicle to use to get people's attention than a Routemaster. It was mostly displayed at Camden Lock Market, where it is seen in these views. Inside the bus, people could look through the collection's image archives, handle some of the collection's objects and watch films from its library. Originally intended to come to an end in December, the Roadshow RML was judged so successful that there were plans at the start of 2014 for further days out with it. (Capital Transport)

ROUTEMASTER COLOURS

The popularity of the Routemaster has meant that they can now be found not only around the United Kingdom but across the world. As an icon of London, most of these have retained their red livery to resemble the traditional London Transport colour scheme.

However, amongst the six hundred and seventy or so Routemasters that survive in the United Kingdom, a minority of examples can be found in non-red livery in a variety of uses.

As would be expected, various examples are preserved by individuals and museums in the green based London Country and Green Line liveries as well as in the liveries of some of the operators that used Routemasters from the mid-1980s onwards.

The previous chapter looked at Routemasters that have been converted to new uses and for promotional work: these are often to be found in special liveries for a particular campaign, although these may by nature only last for a matter of weeks or months. These Routemasters may no longer be in regular passenger carrying service, but some are still fitted out as a bus internally, and have gained non-red liveries for their new owners.

As noted above, they may be in a minority but some Routemasters that are still used and operated in a passenger carrying role have gained a colourful new livery with their new owner. This can, of course, apply to owners based outside the United Kingdom as well.

RMs in another jubilee, that of Her Majesty the Queen in 1977, enter the gates of Buckingham Palace. (London Transport Museum)

Between October 2004 and May 2005 the last production RM, 2217, carried this promotional livery for the 2004 Harry Potter film *Prisoner of Azkaban*. Upon the completion of its promotional work, this RM was restored to pristine condition and used for the final official journey on route 159 on 9th December 2005. (Andrew Morgan)

RM317 is the most southerly Routemaster, based at the southern tip of Argentina; it has been operating the Ushuaia City Tour since 1999 and is often seen meeting the visiting cruise ships. It has been fitted with a Mercedes engine and manual gearbox. Internally it has been fitted with a coffee machine to supply refreshments to its passengers. (Vernon Murphy)

Well known Cornish operator Western Greyhound has three Routemasters in its heritage fleet, but their sole RMA, RMA11, was acquired in 2004 and, unlike the others, it was repainted into fleet livery. (Richard Godfrey)

East Yorkshire operated Routemasters in Hull from May 1988 until August 1995 in a traditional indigo, primrose and white livery. In 1996, RM2065 was converted to open top and, after carrying all over advert liveries, it was repainted into the version of East Yorkshire livery shown below. It is now the sole Routemaster retained by East Yorkshire, and can be often seen in the summer season on the Scarborough sea front. (Richard Godfrey)

RM787 was converted to open top for Somerset based Quantock Motor Services in 2005, a conversion that included an unusual modification of the upper deck side windows. In 2007 the bus passed to York Pullman, being initially used on a sightseeing service in York and more recently on private hire work. (Tony Wilson)

After being withdrawn by London General in 2004, RML2317 was transferred to associate company Metrobus and repainted into Lincoln green livery. In 2009 it passed to Brighton & Hove and was repainted into pseudo Tilling red, cream and grey livery. In memory of a former Brighton resident, and one of the original Routemaster team, this RML was named after Colin Curtis OBE in October 2012. (Richard Godfrey)

The Stratford Blue name was revived in 2002 after Ensignbus took over the former Guide Friday operation in Stratford. In late 2003, RML2565 was repainted in the company's traditional livery complete with adverts for a local brewer. In February 2007, this operation was sold to Stagecoach Midlands, and this RML is subsequently seen in Wellingborough for the centenary celebrations in 2013. (George Gamblin)

RML2570 has been in Ireland since 2008 and it quickly passed to Irish crisp and popcorn manufacturer Tayto. It is seen in this all over advert livery promoting their American-themed activity park which is at Ashbourne to the north west of Dublin. (Andrew Izatt)

RML2288 is seen at the then Blue Triangle depot at Rainham. It was one of two RMLs painted deep blue in 2007 and used as mobile adverts for touring round central London promoting the Daddy Blue show, the other being 2289. They were exported to Germany in this livery, 2289 being sold on at the end of 2013. (Russell Young)

ROUTEMASTER TOURS – 1

MAC TOURS

If someone had suggested, 25 years ago, that Routemasters would be in daily use on Edinburgh's streets in 2014, it would have been dismissed as fantasy. But by the same token, the very idea that Edinburgh's climate could support all-year open-top bus tours would have provoked a similar reaction. But these fantasies become reality each year as Gavin Booth tells us and illustrates.

Lothian Region Transport, now Lothian Buses, was nudged into serious open-top tours when Guide Friday descended on Edinburgh in 1989 and Lothian responded by converting some of its oldest Leyland Atlanteans to open-toppers. Lothian eventually acquired the Guide Friday business but not before another competitor appeared on the scene. A local businessman, Donald Dewar, saw an opportunity to run city tours using vintage buses and bought a variety of older buses for the purpose, operating as Mac Tours, but when he recognised the difficulty of maintaining a mixed, older fleet he started buying former London Routemasters.

In 2002 Lothian Buses acquired the Mac Tours business and the fleet and quickly decided to standardise on Routemasters for the Mac Tours operation. In addition to six acquired with the business, Lothian went out and bought the 10 ERMs, a couple of the 30ft RCL coaches, an RMC and a second forward entrance RMA. The 20-strong fleet now comprised 10 ERM, five RM, two RCL, two RMA and the RMC. All that was missing was an RML, and while Lothian bought two in 2003, these were for spares to allow conversions to semi-open-top layout.

In practice, the 12 fully open-top Routemasters are used at the height of the summer season and in autumn and spring if the weather is suitable, while the five semi-open-toppers are used for the full Mac Tours season.

Although all 20 buses started out as 'pure' AEC-engined Routemasters, concerns over the continuing cost and availability of spares and meeting environmental standards led Lothian to consider re-engining them. All 20 then received Cummins 6BA engines and Allison automatic gearboxes.

Lothian Buses runs four distinct tour brands: City Sightseeing offers pre-recorded commentaries in nine languages and uses red Dennis Tridents; Edinburgh Tour offers a choice of English language commentaries, using green-painted Tridents; Mac Tours offer a live guide, using red/cream Routemasters; and Majestic Tours offer a tour to the north of Edinburgh with a multi-language commentary, and uses blue/yellow Tridents. Although Routemasters are now solely on Mac Tours duties, some have appeared in other liveries for the Edinburgh and Majestic tours.

Kenny Campbell, Lothian's Tour Operations Manager, quickly makes it clear that he is not an enthusiast, so for

him the Routemasters are simply part of the tour fleet he has at his disposal. But he recognises the interest that they create, even though they require a three-person crew – a driver, guide and a conductor-cum-ticket seller. "We recruit a lot of younger people as conductors," says Kenny, "and many don't know what a conductor is."

"Many of the drivers like the Routemasters because they can hear the engine and on Mac Tours they are only required to drive – no buttons to press for recorded commentaries and no tickets to issue en route."

The Routemasters have proved to be reliable buses with very few mechanical problems, although the long wheelbase of the ERMs has caused problems on a few tight turns – often because of badly-parked cars.

The route followed by the Mac Tours Routemasters can be completed in just under an hour, taking in the historic old town of Edinburgh, including part of the Royal Mile, as well as the Georgian New Town, dating from the 18th century. In practice, with delays and diversions in recent years as a result of the tramworks, and the traffic congestion during Festival time in August, plus the marches and processions that disrupt the city centre on a regular basis, the route often has to be changed at short notice. For the 2011 season Lothian extended the times of operation. "We found that many passengers wanted tours later in the afternoon and so we shall be offering departures right up to 19.00hrs," said Kenny Campbell.

A drive of a Mac Tours Routemaster shows that it retains many of the driver-friendly advantages that were designed into the bus from the start, although the noise levels are rather different with the Cummins/Allison drivetrain. There had been comments about engine noise on the re-engined buses, and Lothian worked to suppress noise with an insulated bonnet. Engineers found that the noise levels on the Cummins were the same as the AEC, but because the AEC was a heavy engine it absorbed much of the noise itself. The B series is much lighter and sets up more resonance. In fact once the bus is in top gear what you hear is more of a gentle burble. The trick, it seems, is to get it quickly into top gear, then reduce speed – and it usually holds the gear without dropping down to third. Much of the Mac Tours operation involves slow speeds in heavy traffic and the gearbox settings reflect this.

The cab layout is rather different now. There are still controls above the driver's nearside window, but these are for side/head lights, demister, wipers and washers. To the right of the steering column is the direction indicator and a new row of warning lights – red for alternator, orange for oil pressure, green for low water and blue for high temperature. A modern-style starter switch is positioned beside the lights.

To the left of the steering column is the Allison gear selector, which is not a conventional gear control. It is a pad with buttons for reverse, neutral and drive, and a mode selector that allows the driver to select lower gears using buttons with arrows. The appropriate gear is shown in a display on the panel. Pressing drive shows '4', and you can happily leave it in this position for normal driving. But if you want to keep the bus in lower gears, you can select these and it won't change to a gear higher than the one displayed.

The Mac Tours Routemasters seem to have a secure future, particularly following the experimental fitment of an SCRT system to the exhaust of ERM163, which reduces pollutants and effectively takes a 50-year old bus to Euro V standard. In their nine-month season the Mac Tours Routemasters make an important contribution to Lothian's tour total of half a million passengers per year. The Mac fleet now sits at 13 buses – the ERMs and RCLs and one Routemaster (the other seven were sold in 2009) – but the Mac Tours brand is now well established and the fleet still has life in it, a tribute to the soundness of the original design.

ROUTEMASTER TOURS – 2

THE GHOST BUS

You may have seen a black Routemaster running along a Central London Street. This is the Ghost Bus. Intrepid Mark Kehoe volunteered to go on a tour in it.

In 2009, a new tour commenced in London as the Necrobus Ghost Bus Tour. This was the first Ghost bus tour in the world and others are now appearing in many other haunts in cities around the United Kingdom. And in case you were wondering, Necro is Latin for 'the dead'.

Using a Routemaster, the London tour is the combination of theatrical performance and tales of haunted London passing through the locations of many historical sources of London's ghoulish past. It starts near Trafalgar Square at Northumberland Avenue and runs to Parliament Square, then returns to the Strand and enters the City of London, Smithfield, Tower, and stops at a location near Stamford Street. Here the curtains are closed across the windows so for a while you do not know where you are. Later in the tour, it stops and all the passengers are shown a site full of bones which are alleged to be so haunted that no-one will develop the site.

The crew are actors who rather than pass time waiting in cafes and restaurants, hone their skills by placing passengers on the edge of their bus seats and wondering if they should have taken the number 11 instead.

Internally the bus has been retrimmed to resemble a Victorian funeral parlour, with lots of burgundy, leather chesterfield style studded seats, curtains and chintzy table lamps. The bus has smoke effects, well positioned TV monitors and cameras, and a very good sound system. All are used to good effect as strange things happen on this bus.

The conductor is one of the actors but he stays in character throughout as a rather nervy but reassuring tour guide. Another actor or two appear during the tour, one as the Health and Safety inspector for the bus operator, who can feel something terrible on the bus. It is all very funny in a slightly unnerving way, but it is probably best that some of this entertainment is left for you to find out. The bus is driven by a very experienced bus driver and this particular bus, RML2516, is very quiet, smooth and has a swift turn of speed.

So this tour is not your average sightseeing tour – the Ghost Bus Tours website describes it as a *Frightseeing tour like no other ... designed to entertain and educate while providing a spooky theatrical experience you'll never forget* – and that is what this tour definitely is.

Pictured is Oliver Malam, a tour guide on the Ghost Bus. Note the blinds on the RML.

Right Inside the Ghost Bus in between tours.

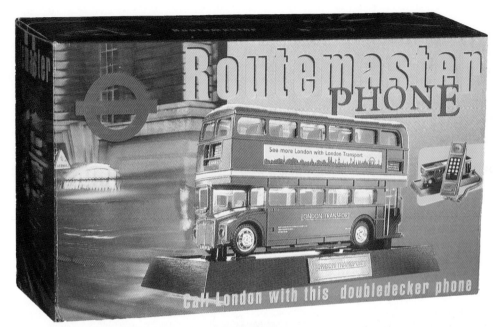

Innumerable souvenirs and models of the Routemaster have been produced over the years. We began the book with a child's jigsaw puzzle produced in the late 1950s. A 1970s item is this fully working Routemaster desk phone. (Capital Transport)